A Brief Introduction to Buddhism

D1613740

A Brief Introduction to
BUDDHISM

Updated and revised by Tim Dowley
General Editor: Christopher Partridge

Fortress Press
Minneapolis

A BRIEF INTRODUCTION TO BUDDHISM

Copyright © 2018 Fortress Press. All rights reserved. Except for brief quotations
in critical articles or reviews, no part of this book may be reproduced in any manner
without prior written permission from the publisher. Email copyright@1517.media or
write to Permissions, Fortress Press, PO Box 1209, Minneapolis, MN 55440-1209.

Scripture quotations marked NIV are from the Holy Bible, New International Version
copyright © 1973, 1978, 1984 International Bible Society. Used by permission of
Zondervan and Hodder & Stoughton Limited. All rights reserved. The 'NIV' and
'New International Version' trademarks are registered in the United States Patent and
Trademark Office by International Bible Society. Use of either trademark requires the
permission of International Bible Society. UK trademark 1448790.

Scripture quotations marked Good News Bible are from the Good News Bible (GNB)
© American Bible Society 1966, 1971, 1976.

Scripture quotations marked Revised Standard Version is taken from the Revised
Standard Version of the Bible, copyright 1952 2nd edition, 1971 by the Division of
Christian Education of the National Council of Churches of Christ in the United
States of America. Used by permission. All rights reserved. Scripture quotations
marked KJV are from the King James Version.

The maps and images on pages 90-95 appear in *Atlas of World Religions*
(Fortress Press, forthcoming).

Cover image: Mandala/iStock.com/Volker Göllner; Buddha Face/iStock.com/
Maodesign
Cover design: Laurie Ingram

Print ISBN: 978-1-5064-5030-8
eBook ISBN: 978-1-5064-5031-5

The paper used in this publication meets the minimum requirements of American
National Standard for Information Sciences — Permanence of Paper for Printed
Library Materials, ANSI Z329.48-1984.

Manufactured in the U.SA

CONSULTING EDITORS

Dr Veikko Anttonen
Professor of Comparative Religion,
School of Cultural Research,
University of Turku, Finland

Dr Eric S. Christianson
Formerly Senior Lecturer in Biblical Studies,
University College Chester, UK

Dr Diana L. Eck
Professor of Comparative Religion and
Indian Studies, Harvard Divinity School,
Cambridge, MA, USA

Dr Gavin Flood
Professor of Hindu Studies and
Comparative Religion,
University of Oxford, UK

Dr Andreas Grünschloß
Professor of Religious Studies,
Göttingen University, Germany

Dr Robert J. Kisala,
Associate Professor, Nanzan University,
Nagoya, Japan

Dr Anthony N. S. Lane
Professor of Historical Theology and
Director of Research,
London School of Theology, UK

Dr Nicholas de Lange
Professor of Hebrew and Jewish Studies,
University of Cambridge, UK

Dr Mikael Rothstein
Associate Professor of Religious History,
University of Copenhagen, Denmark

Professor Lamin Sanneh
D. Willis James Professor of Missions and
World Christianity and Professor of History,
Yale Divinity School, New Haven, CT, USA

Baron Singh of Wimbledon CBE

Dr Garry W. Trompf
Emeritus Professor in the History of Ideas,
University of Sydney, Australia

Dr Linda Woodhead
Professor of Sociology of Religion,
Lancaster University, UK

Contents

PART 1
UNDERSTANDING RELIGION

PART 2
BUDDHISM

Contributors

Dr Barbara M. Boal, formerly Lecturer in Primal Religions, Selly Oak Colleges, Birmingham, UK: *The Cao Dai and the Hoa Hoa*

Dr Fiona Bowie, Honorary Research Fellow, Department of Archaeology and Anthropology, University of Bristol, UK: *The Anthropology of Religion, Ritual and Performance*

Dr Jeremy Carrette, Professor of Religion and Culture, University of Kent, England: *Critical Theory and Religion*

Dr Douglas Davies, Professor in the Study of Religion, Department of Theology and Religion, University of Durham, UK: *Myths and Symbols*

Dr Malcolm Hamilton, Senior Lecturer, Department of Sociology, University of Reading, UK: *The Sociology of Religion*

Dr Elizabeth J. Harris, Senior Lecturer, Comparative Study of Religions, Liverpool Hope University, UK: *Buddhism: Beliefs, Family and Society, Buddhism in the Modern World*

Dr Paul Hedges, Senior Lecturer in Theology and Religious Studies: *Theological Approaches to the Study of Religion*

Magdalen Lambkin, PhD, University of Glasgow, Scotland: Consultant, *Understanding Religion*

Dr Russell T. McCutcheon, Professor of Sociology of Religion, University of Alabama, USA: *What is Religion?*

Dr Christopher Partridge, Professor of Religious Studies, University of Lancaster, UK: *Phenomenology and the Study of Religion, Rapid Fact-finder*

Paul Seto: *I am a Buddhist*

Revd Angela Tilby, Diocesan Canon, Christ Church, Oxford, UK: *Rapid Fact-finder*

Dr Fraser N. Watts, Starbridge Lecturer in Theology and Natural Science, University of Cambridge, UK: *The Psychology of Religion*

Dr Paul Williams, Emeritus Professor of Indian and Tibetan Philosophy, University of Bristol, UK: *Buddhism: A Historical Overview, Sacred Writings*

Revd Dr John-David Yule, Incumbent of the United Benefice of Fen Drayton with Conington, Lolworth, and Swavesey, Cambridge, UK: *Rapid Fact-finder*

List of Maps

List of Time Charts

List of Illustrations

Preface

This volume and five other titles in the *Brief Introductions* series are taken directly from the third edition of *Introduction to World Religions*, edited by Christopher Partridge and revised by Tim Dowley. Additional maps and images are included from *Atlas of World Religions*, edited by Tim Dowley. We recognized that smaller volumes focused on specific religious traditions might be especially helpful for use in corresponding religious studies courses. General readers who are eager to know and understand more about religious beliefs and practices will find this series to be an engaging and accessible way to explore the world's religions—one by one.

Other Books in the Series
A Brief Introduction to Christianity
A Brief Introduction to Hinduism
A Brief Introduction to Islam
A Brief Introduction to Jainism and Sikhism
A Brief Introduction to Judaism

PART I
UNDERSTANDING RELIGION

SUMMARY

Belief in something that exists beyond or outside our understanding – whether spirits, gods, or simply a particular order to the world – has been present at every stage in the development of human society, and has been a major factor in shaping much of that development. Unsurprisingly, many have devoted themselves to the study of religion, whether to understand a particular set of beliefs, or to explain why humans seem instinctively drawn to religion. While biologists, for example, may seek to understand what purpose religion served in our evolutionary descent, we are concerned here with the beliefs, rituals, and speculation about existence that we – with some reservation – call religion.

The question of what 'religion' actually is is more fraught than might be expected. Problems can arise when we try to define the boundaries between religion and philosophy when speculation about existence is involved, or between religion and politics when moral teaching or social structure are at issue. In particular, once we depart from looking at the traditions of the West, many contend that such apparently obvious distinctions should not be applied automatically.

While there have always been people interested in the religious traditions of others, such 'comparative' approaches are surprisingly new. Theology faculties are among the oldest in European universities, but, while the systematic internal exploration of a religion provides considerable insights, many scholars insisted that the examination of religions more generally should be conducted instead by objective observers. This phenomenological approach was central to the establishment of the study of religion as a discipline in its own right. Others, concerned with the nature of society, or the workings of the human mind, for example, were inevitably drawn to the study of religion to expand their respective areas. More recently, many have attempted to utilise the work of these disparate approaches. In particular, many now suggest that – because no student can ever be entirely objective – theological studies are valuable because of their ability to define a religion in its own terms: by engaging with this alongside other, more detached, approaches, a student may gain a more accurate view of a particular religion.

CHAPTER I

What Is Religion?

Although no one is certain of the word's origins, we know that 'religion' derives from Latin, and that languages influenced by Latin have equivalents to the English word 'religion'. In Germany, the systematic study of religion is known as *Religionswissenschaft*, and in France as *les sciences religieuses*. Although the ancient words to which we trace 'religion' have nothing to do with today's meanings — it may have come from the Latin word that meant to tie something tightly (*religare*) — it is today commonly used to refer to those beliefs, behaviours, and social institutions which have something to do with speculations on any, and all, of the following: the origin, end, and significance of the universe; what happens after death; the existence and wishes of powerful, non-human beings such as spirits, ancestors, angels, demons, and gods; and the manner in which all of this shapes human behaviour.

Because each of these makes reference to an invisible (that is, non-empirical) world that somehow lies outside of, or beyond, human history, the things we name as 'religious' are commonly thought to be opposed to those institutions which we label as 'political'. In the West today we generally operate under the assumption that, whereas religion is a matter of personal belief that can never be settled by rational debate, such things as politics are observable, public, and thus open to rational debate.

THE ESSENCE OF 'RELIGION'

Although this commonsense distinction between private and public, sentiment and action, is itself a historical development — it is around the seventeenth century that we first see evidence that words that once referred to one's behaviour, public standing, and social rank (such as piety and reverence) became sentimentalized as matters of private feeling — today the assumption that religion involves an inner core of belief that is somehow expressed publicly in ritual is so widespread that to question it appears counterintuitive. It is just this assumption that inspires a number of people who, collectively, we could term 'essentialists'. They are 'essentialists' because they maintain that 'religion' names the outward behaviours that are inspired by the inner thing they call 'faith'. Hence, one can imagine someone saying, 'I'm not religious, but I'm spiritual.' Implicit here is the assumption that the institutions associated with religions — hierarchies, regulations, rituals, and so on — are merely secondary and inessential; the important thing is the inner faith, the inner 'essence' of religion. Although the essence of religion – the thing without which someone is thought to be non-religious – is known by various names (faith, belief, the Sacred, the Holy, and so on), essentialists are in general agreement that the essence of religion is real and non-empirical (that is, it cannot itself be seen, heard, touched, and so on); it defies study and must be experienced first-hand.

THE FUNCTION OF 'RELIGION'

Apart from an approach that assumes an inner experience, which underlies religious behaviour, scholars have used the term 'religion' for what they consider to be curious areas of observable human behaviour which require an explanation. Such people form theories to account for why it is people think, for example, that an invisible part of their body, usually called 'the soul', outlives that body; that powerful beings control the universe; and that there is more to existence than what is observable. These theories are largely functionalist; that is, they seek to determine the social, psychological, or political role played by the things we refer to as 'religious'. Such functionalists include historically:

- Karl Marx (1818–83), whose work in political economy understood religion to be a pacifier that deadened oppressed people's sense of pain and alienation, while simultaneously preventing them from doing something about their lot in life, since ultimate responsibility was thought to reside in a being who existed outside history.

Karl Marx (1818–83).

- Émile Durkheim (1858–1917), whose sociology defined religious as sets of beliefs and practices to enable individuals who engaged in them to form a shared, social identity.
- Sigmund Freud (1856–1939), whose psychological studies prompted him to liken religious behaviour to the role that dreams play in helping people to vent antisocial anxieties in a manner that does not threaten their place within the group.

Although these classic approaches are all rather different, each can be understood as *functionalist* insomuch as religion names an institution that has a role to play in helping individuals and communities to reproduce themselves.

THE FAMILY RESEMBLANCE APPROACH

Apart from the *essentialist* way of defining religion (i.e. there is some non-empirical, core feature without which something is not religious) and the *functionalist* (i.e. that religions help to satisfy human needs), there is a third approach: the *family resemblance* definition. Associated with the philosophy of Ludwig Wittgenstein (1889–1951), a family resemblance approach assumes that nothing is defined by merely one essence or function. Rather, just as members of a family more or less share a series of traits, and just as all things we call 'games' more or less share a series of traits – none of which is distributed evenly across all members of those groups we call 'family' or 'games' – so all things – including religion – are defined insomuch as they more or less share a series of delimited traits. Ninian Smart (1927–2001), who identified seven dimensions of religion that are present in religious traditions with varying degrees of emphasis, is perhaps the best known proponent of this view.

'RELIGION' AS CLASSIFIER

Our conclusion is that the word 'religion' likely tells us more about the user of the word (i.e. the classifier) than it does about the thing being classified. For instance, a Freudian psychologist will not conclude that religion functions to oppress the masses, since the Freudian theory precludes coming up with this Marxist conclusion. On the other hand, a scholar who adopts Wittgenstein's approach will sooner or later come up with a case in which something seems to share some traits, but perhaps not enough to count as 'a religion'. If, say, soccer matches satisfy many of the criteria of a religion, what might not also be called religion if soccer is? And what does such a broad usage do to the specificity, and thus utility, of the word 'religion'? As for those who adopt an essentialist approach, it is likely no coincidence that only those institutions with which one agrees are thought to be expressions of some authentic inner experience, sentiment, or emotion, whilst the traditions of others are criticized as being shallow and derivative.

So what is religion? As with any other item in our lexicon, 'religion' is a historical artefact that different social actors use for different purposes: to classify certain parts of their social world in order to celebrate, degrade, or theorize about them. Whatever else it may or may not be, religion is at least an item of rhetoric that group members use to sort out their group identities.

RUSSELL T. MCCUTCHEON

CHAPTER 2

Phenomenology and the Study of Religion

There is a long history of curiosity and scholarship regarding the religions of other people. However, the study of religions is a relative newcomer to academia. Greatly indebted to the impressive work and influence of the German scholar Friedrich Max Müller (1823–1900), the first university professorships were established in the final quarter of the nineteenth century. By the second half of the twentieth century, the study of religion had emerged as an important field of academic enquiry. In a period of history during which the rationalism of the earlier part of the century saw a decline, and in which there was increased interest in particularly non-Christian spirituality, since 1945 there has been a growth in courses in the study of religion offered in academic institutions. Moreover, work done in other disciplines has increasingly converged with the work done by students of religion (see the discussion in this book of 'The Anthropology of Religion', 'The Psychology of Religion', 'The Sociology of Religion', and 'Critical Theory and Religion').

These factors, amongst others, have made it possible for the study of religion in most Western universities to pull away from its traditional place alongside the study of Christian theology and establish itself as an independent field of enquiry. Whereas earlier in the century the study of non-Christian faiths was usually undertaken in faculties of Christian theology, and studied as part of a theology degree, there was a move – particularly in the late 1960s and 1970s, when the term 'religious studies' became common currency – to establish separate departments of religious studies. Whilst in the United States and most of Western Europe religious studies tends to be considered a subject completely distinct from theology, in the United Kingdom it is quite common for universities to offer degree programmes in 'theology and religious studies', and the lines between the two disciplines are not so heavily drawn.

RELIGIONSPHÄNOMENOLOGIE

Phenomenology is distinct from other approaches to the study of religion in that it does not necessarily seek to understand the social nature of religion, it is not concerned to explore the psychological factors involved in religious belief, nor is it

especially interested in the historical development of religions. Rather its main concern has been descriptive, the classification of religious phenomena: objects, rituals, teachings, behaviours, and so on.

During the Kumbh Mela festival in the holy city of Haridwar the Guru in his decorated chariot is escorted by holy men and pilgrims visiting the River Ganges, India.

The term *Religionsphänomenologie* was first used by the Dutch scholar Pierre Daniel Chantepie de la Saussaye (1848–1920) in his work *Lehrbuch der Religions-geschichte* (1887), which simply documented religious phenomena. This might be described as 'descriptive' phenomenology, the aim being to gather information about the various religions and, as botanists might classify plants, identify varieties of particular religious phenomena. This classification of types of religious phenomena, the hallmark of the phenomenological method, can be seen in the works of scholars such as Ninian Smart (1927–2001) and Mircea Eliade (1907–86). Descriptive phenomenology of the late nineteenth and early twentieth centuries tended to lead to accounts of religious phenomena which, to continue with the analogy, read much the same as a botanical handbook. Various species were identified (higher religion, lower religion, prophetic religion, mystical religion, and so on) and particular religious beliefs and practices were then categorized, discussed, and compared.

As the study of religion progressed, phenomenology came to refer to a method which was more complex, and claimed rather more for itself, than Chantepie's mere

A BRIEF INTRODUCTION TO BUDDHISM

cataloguing of facts. This later development in the discipline – which was due in part to the inspiration of the philosophy of Edmund Husserl (1859–1938) – recognized how easy it is for prior beliefs and interpretations unconsciously to influence one's thinking. Hence, scholars such as Gerardus van der Leeuw (1890–1950) stressed the need for phenomenological *epoché*: the 'bracketing' or shelving of the question about the ontological or objective status of the religious appearances to consciousness. Thus questions about the objective or independent truth of Kali, Allah, or the Holy Spirit are initially laid aside. The scholar seeks to suspend judgment about the beliefs of those he studies in order to gain greater objectivity and accuracy in understanding. Also central to phenomenology is the need for empathy (*Einfühlung*), which helps towards an understanding of the religion from within. Students of a religion seek to feel their way into the beliefs of others by empathizing with them. Along with this suspension of judgment and empathy, phenomenologists spoke of 'eidetic vision', the capacity of the observer to see beyond the particularities of a religion and to grasp its core essence and meaning. Whilst we often see only what we want, or expect, to see, eidetic vision is the ability to see a phenomenon without such distortions and limitations. Hence, later phenomenologists did not merely catalogue the facts of religious history, but by means of *epoché*, empathy, and eidetic vision sought to understand their meaning for the believer. Although phenomenologists are well aware that there will always be some distance between the believer's understandings of religious facts and those of the scholar, the aim of phenomenology is, as far as possible, to testify only to what has been observed. It aims to strip away all that would stand in the way of a neutral, judgment-free presentation of the facts.

THE IDEA OF THE HOLY

> '*Numinous dread*' or awe characterizes the so-called '*religion of primitive man*', where it appears as '*daemonic dread.*'
>
> Rudolf Otto, *The Idea of the Holy*

Some scholars have gone beyond this simple presentation of the facts and claimed more. A classic example is Rudolf Otto's (1869–1937) book *Das Heilige* (*The Idea of the Holy*, 1917). On the basis of his study of religions, Otto claimed that central to all religious expression is an a priori sense of 'the numinous' or 'the holy'. This, of course, necessarily goes beyond a simple presentation of the facts of religious history to the development of a particular philosophical interpretation of those facts. The central truth of all religion, claimed Otto, is a genuine feeling of awe or reverence in the believer, a sense of the 'uncanny' inspired by an encounter with the divine. Otto did more than simply relate facts about religion; he assumed the existence of the holy – accepting the truth of encounters with the supernatural.

For some scholars, for example Ninian Smart, such an assumption is unacceptable in the study of religion. To compromise objectivity in this way, Smart argued, skews the scholar's research and findings. What the scholar ends up with is not an unbiased account of the facts of religion, but a personal *theology* of religion.

NEUTRALITY

Whilst Otto's type of phenomenology clearly displays a basic lack of objectivity, it is now generally recognized that this is a problem intrinsic to the study of religions. Although many contemporary religious studies scholars would want to defend the notion of *epoché* as an ideal to which one should aspire, there is a question as to whether this ideal involves a certain naivety. For example, the very process of selection and production of typologies assumes a level of interpretation. To select certain facts rather than others, and to present them with other facts as a particular type of religion, presupposes some interpretation. What facts we consider important and unimportant, interesting or uninteresting, will be shaped by certain ideas that we hold, whether religious or non-religious. To be an atheist does not in itself make the scholar more objective and neutral. Hence, the belief in detached objectivity, and the claim to be purely 'descriptive', are now considered to be naive. The important thing is that, as we engage in study, we recognize and critically evaluate our beliefs, our presuppositions, our biases, and how they might shape the way we understand a religion (see 'Critical Theory and Religion').

INSIDERS AND OUTSIDERS

Another important issue in contemporary religious studies is the 'insider/outsider' problem. To what extent can a non-believer ('an outsider') understand a faith in the way the believer (an 'insider') does? It is argued that outsiders, simply because they are outsiders, will never fully grasp the insider's experience; even people who experience the same event at the same time will, because of their contexts and personal histories, interpret that experience in different ways. However, some scholars have insisted there is a definite advantage to studying religion from the outside – sometimes referred to as the 'etic' perspective. Members of a religion may be conditioned by, or pressurized into accepting, a particular – and often narrow – understanding of their faith, whereas the outsider is in the scholarly position of not being influenced by such pressures and conditioning. Impartiality and disinterest allow greater objectivity.

There is undoubtedly value in scholarly detachment. However – while the scholar may have a greater knowledge of the history, texts, philosophy, structure, and social implications of a particular faith than the average believer – not to have experienced that faith from the inside is surely to have a rather large hole in the centre of one's understanding. Indeed, many insiders will insist that scholarly 'head-knowledge' is peripheral to the 'meaning' of their faith. Hence, others have noted the value of studying a religion as an 'insider', or at least relying heavily on the views of insiders – sometimes referred to as the 'emic' perspective.

RESPONSE THRESHOLD

In order to take account of the emic perspective, along with the emphasis on participant observation (see 'The Anthropology of Religion'), some have spoken of the 'response threshold' in religious studies. The crossing of the response threshold happens when insiders question the scholar's interpretations: etic interpretations are challenged by emic perspectives. An insider's perspective – which may conflict with scholarly interpretations – is felt to carry equal, if not more, weight. Wilfred Cantwell Smith (1916–2000) has even argued that no understanding of a faith is valid until it has been acknowledged by an insider. Religious studies are thus carried out in the context of a dialogue which takes seriously the views of the insider, in order to gain a deeper understanding of the insider's world view.

BEYOND PHENOMENOLOGY

In his book entitled *Beyond Phenomenology* (1999), Gavin Flood has argued that what is important in studying religions is 'not so much the distinction between the insider and the outsider, but between the critical and the non-critical'. Flood makes use of theories developed within the social sciences and humanities. With reference to the shift in contemporary theoretical discourse, which recognizes that all knowledge is tradition-specific and embodied within particular cultures (see 'Critical Theory and Religion'), Flood argues, firstly, that religions should not be abstracted and studied apart from the historical, political, cultural, linguistic, and social contexts. Secondly, he argues that scholars, who are likewise shaped by their own contexts, always bring conceptual baggage to the study of religion. Hence, whether because of the effect research has on the community being studied, or because the scholar's own prejudices, preconceptions, instincts, emotions, and personal characteristics significantly influence that research, the academic study of religion can never be neutral and purely objective. Flood thus argues for 'a rigorous metatheoretical discourse' in religious studies. Metatheory is the critical analysis of theory and practice, the aim of which is to 'unravel the underlying assumptions inherent in any research programme and to critically comment on them'.

Metatheory is thus important because it 'questions the contexts of inquiry, the nature of inquiry, and the kinds of interests represented in inquiry'. In so doing, it questions the idea of detached objectivity in the study of religion, and the notion that one can be a disinterested observer who is able to produce neutral descriptions of religious phenomena, free of evaluative judgments. Hence, scholars need always to engage critically with, and take account of, their own assumptions, prejudices, and presuppositions.

This means that holding a particular faith need not be a hindrance to the study of religion. One can, for example, be a Christian theologian and a good student of religion. But for scholars such as Flood, the important thing is not the faith or lack of it, but the awareness of, and the critical engagement with, one's assumptions: 'It is critique rather than faith that is all important.'

It is worth noting that recent work, mainly in France, sees new possibilities for the philosophy of religion through a turn to phenomenology. Much of this work has been done in response to the important French Jewish philosopher Emmanuel Levinas (1905–95). The names particularly associated with this turn are Jean-Luc Marion, Dominique Janicaud, Jean-Luc Chretien, Michel Henry, and Alain Badiou. Marion, for example, has written on the phenomenology of the gift in theology, Badiou has responded to Levinas arguing against his emphasis on the importance of 'the other', and Chretien has written on the phenomenology of prayer.

CHRISTOPHER PARTRIDGE

CHAPTER 3

The Anthropology of Religion

Anthropology approaches religion as an aspect of culture. Religious beliefs and practices are important because they are central to the ways in which we organize our social lives. They shape our understanding of our place in the world, and determine how we relate to one another and to the rest of the natural, and supernatural, order. The truth or falsity of religious beliefs, or the authenticity or moral worth of religious practices, are seldom an issue for anthropologists, whose main concern is to document what people think and do, rather than determine what they ought to believe, or how they should behave.

RELIGION AND SOCIAL STRUCTURE

An early observation in the anthropology of religion was the extent to which religion and social structure mirror one another. Both the French historian Fustel de Coulanges (1830–89), drawing on Classical sources, and the Scottish biblical scholar William Robertson Smith (1846–94), who studied Semitic religions, demonstrated this coincidence in form. For example, nomadic peoples such as the Bedouin conceive of God in terms

> *The belief in a supreme God or a single God is no mere philosophical speculation; it is a great practical idea.*
>
> Maurice Hocart

of a father, and use familial and pastoral imagery to describe their relationship with God. A settled, hierarchical society, by contrast, will depict God as a monarch to whom tribute is due, with imagery of servants and subjects honouring a supreme ruler. These early studies influenced the French sociologist Émile Durkheim (1858–1917), whose book *The Elementary Forms of the Religious Life* (1912) was foundational for later anthropological studies of religion. Rather than seeing religion as determining social structure, Durkheim argued that religion is a projection of society's highest values and goals. The realm of the sacred is separated from the profane world and made to seem both natural and obligatory. Through collective rituals people both reaffirm their belief in supernatural beings and reinforce their bonds with one another.

The totemism of Australian Aboriginals, which links human groups with particular forms of animal or other natural phenomena in relations of prohibition and prescription, was regarded by many nineteenth-century scholars as the earliest form of religion, and as such was of interest to both Durkheim and the anthropologist Edward Burnett Tylor

(1832–1917), who postulated an evolutionary movement from animism to polytheism and then monotheism. However, as evolutionary arguments are essentially unprovable, later work built not on these foundations, but on the more sociological insights of Durkheim and anthropologists such as Alfred Radcliffe-Brown (1881–1955) and Sir Edward Evan Evans-Pritchard (1902–73).

Evans-Pritchard sought to retain the historical perspective of his predecessors, while replacing speculation concerning origins with data based on first-hand observations and participation in the life of a people. His classic 1937 ethnography of witchcraft, oracles, and magic among the Azande in Central Africa demonstrated that beliefs which, from a Western perspective, appear irrational and unscientific — such as the existence of witches and magic — are perfectly logical, once one understands the ideational system on which a society is based.

SYMBOLISM

While Durkheim was avowedly atheist, some of the most influential anthropologists of the later twentieth century, including Evans-Pritchard, were or became practising Roman Catholics. This is true of Mary Douglas (1921–2007) and Victor Turner (1920–83), both of whom were particularly interested in the symbolic aspects of religion. They were influenced not only by Durkheim and Evans-Pritchard, but more particularly by Durkheim's gifted pupils Marcel Mauss (1872–1950) and Henri Hubert (1864–1925), who wrote on ceremonial exchange, sacrifice, and magic.

> *Man is an animal suspended in webs of significance he himself has spun. I take culture to be those webs.*
>
> Clifford Geertz, *The Interpretation of Cultures: Selected Essays* (New York, 1973)

In her influential collection of essays *Purity and Danger* (1966), Douglas looked at the ways in which the human body is used as a symbol system in which meanings are encoded. The body is seen as a microcosm of the powers and dangers attributed to society at large. Thus, a group that is concerned to maintain its social boundaries, such as members of the Brahman caste in India, pays great attention to notions of purity and pollution as they affect the individual body. In examining purity rules, Douglas was primarily concerned with systems of classification. In her study of the Hebrew purity rules in the book of Leviticus, for example, Douglas argued that dietary proscriptions were not the result of medical or hygiene concerns, but followed the logic of a system of classification that divided animals into clean and unclean species according to whether they conformed to certain rules — such as being cloven-hooved and chewing cud — or were anomalous, and therefore unclean and prohibited. Like Robertson Smith, Douglas observed that rituals can retain their form over many generations, notwithstanding changes in their interpretation, and that meaning is preserved in the form itself, as well as in explanations for a particular ritual action.

In the work of Mary Douglas we see a fruitful combination of the sociological and symbolist tradition of the Durkheimians and the structuralism of Claude Lévi-Strauss (1908–2009). Lévi-Strauss carried out some fieldwork in the Amazonian region of Brazil, but it is as a theoretician that he has been most influential, looking not at the meaning or semantics of social structure, but at its syntax or formal aspects. In his four-volume study of mythology (1970–81), he sought to demonstrate the universality of certain cultural themes, often expressed as binary oppositions, such as the transformation of food from raw to cooked, or the opposition between culture and nature. The structuralism of Lévi-Strauss both looks back to Russian formalism and the linguistics of the Swiss Ferdinand de Saussure (1857–1913), and forwards to more recent psychoanalytic studies of religion, both of which see themselves as belonging more to a scientific than to a humanist tradition.

RITUAL AND SYMBOL

On the symbolist and interpretive side, Victor Turner (1920–83) produced a series of sensitive, detailed studies of ritual and symbols, focusing on the processual nature of ritual and its theatrical, dramatic aspects, based on extensive fieldwork among the Ndembu of Zambia carried out in the 1950s. Clifford Geertz (1926–2006) was equally concerned with meaning and interpretation, and following a German-American tradition he looked more at culture than at social structure. Geertz saw religion as essentially that which gives meaning to human society, and religious symbols as codifying an ethos or world view. Their power lies in their ability both to reflect and to shape society.

Recently, important changes have stemmed from postmodernism and postcolonial thinking, globalization and multiculturalism. Anthropologists now often incorporate a critique of their own position and interests into their studies, and are no longer preoccupied exclusively with 'exotic' small-scale societies; for instance, there is a lot of research into global Pentecostalism and its local forms. The impact of new forms of media in the religious sphere has also become a significant area of study.

FIONA BOWIE

MYTHS AND SYMBOLS

One dimension of religions which has received particular attention by scholars has been that of myths and symbols. If we had just heard a moving piece of music, we would find it strange if someone asked us whether the music were true or false. Music, we might reply, is neither true nor false; to ask such a question is inappropriate. Most people know that music can, as it were, speak to them, even though no words are used.

As with music so with people. The question of what someone 'means' to you cannot fully be answered by saying that he is your husband or she is your wife, because there are always unspoken levels of intuition, feeling, and emotion built into relationships. The question of 'meaning' must always be seen to concern these dimensions, as well as the more obviously factual ones.

Myths

Myths take many forms, depending on the culture in which they are found. But their function is always that of pinpointing vital issues and values in the life of the society concerned. They often dramatize those profound issues of life and death, of how humanity came into being, and of what life means, of how we should conduct ourselves as a citizen or spouse, as a creature of God or as a farmer, and so on.

Myths are not scientific or sociological theories about these issues; they are the outcome of the way a nation or group has pondered the great questions. Their function is not merely to provide a theory of life that can be taken or left at will; they serve to compel a response from humanity. We might speak of myths as bridges between the intellect and emotion, between the mind and heart – and in this, myths are like music. They express an idea and trigger our response to it.

Sometimes myths form an extensive series, interlinking with each other and encompassing many aspects of life, as has been shown for the Dogon people of the River Niger in West Africa. On the other hand, they may serve merely as partial accounts of problems, such as the hatred between people and snakes, or the reason for the particular shape of a mountain.

One problem in our understanding of myths lies in the fact that the so-called Western religions – Judaism, Christianity, and Islam – are strongly concerned with history. They have founders, and see their history as God's own doing. This strong emphasis upon actual events differs from the Eastern approaches to religion, which emphasize the consciousness of the individual. Believing in the cyclical nature of time, Hinduism and Buddhism possess a different approach to history, and hence also to science.

In the West, the search for facts in science is like the search for facts in history, but both these endeavours differ from the search for religious experience in the present. In the West, history and science have come to function as a framework within which religious experiences are found and interpreted, one consequence of which is that myths are often no longer appreciated for their power to evoke human responses to religious ideas.

The eminent historian of religion Mircea Eliade (1907–86) sought to restore this missing sense of the sacred by helping people to understand the true nature of myths. The secularized Westerner has lost the sense of the sacred, and is trying to compensate, as Eliade saw it, by means of science fiction, supernatural literature, and films. One may, of course, keep a firm sense of history and science without seeking to destroy the mythical appreciation of ideas and beliefs.

Symbols

Religious symbols help believers to understand their faith in quite profound ways. Like myths, they serve to unite the intellect and the emotions. Symbols also integrate the social and personal dimensions of religion, enabling individuals to share certain commonly held beliefs expressed by symbols, while also giving freedom to read private meaning into them.

We live the whole of our life in a world of symbols. The daily smiles and grimaces, handshakes and greetings, as well as the more readily acknowledged status symbols of large cars or houses – all these communicate messages about ourselves to others.

To clarify the meaning of symbols, it will help if we distinguish between the terms 'symbol' and 'sign'. There is a certain arbitrariness about signs, so that the word 'table', which signifies an object of furniture with a flat top supported on legs, could be swapped for another sound without any difficulty. Thus the Germans call it *tisch* and the Welsh *bwrdd*.

A symbol, by contrast, is more intimately involved in that to which it refers. It participates in what it symbolizes, and cannot easily be swapped for another symbol. Nor can it be explained in words and still carry the same power. For example, a kiss is a symbol of affection and love; it not only signifies these feelings in some abstract way; it actually demonstrates them. In this sense a symbol can be a thought in action.

Religious symbols share these general characteristics, but are often even more intensely powerful, because they enshrine and express the highest values and relationships of life. The cross of Christ, the sacred books of Muslims and Sikhs, the sacred cow of Hindus, or the silent, seated Buddha – all these command the allegiance of millions of religious men and women. If such symbols are attacked or desecrated, an intense reaction is felt by the faithful, which shows us how deeply symbols are embedded in the emotional life of believers.

The power of symbols lies in this ability to unite fellow-believers into a community. It provides a focal point of faith and action, while also making possible a degree of personal understanding which those outside may not share.

In many societies the shared aspect of symbols is important as a unifying principle of life. Blood, for example, may be symbolic of life, strength, parenthood, or of the family and kinship group itself. In Christianity it expresses life poured out in death, the self-sacrificial love of Christ who died for human sin. It may even be true that the colour red can so easily serve as a symbol of

The cross is the central symbol of Christianity.

danger because of its deeper biological association with life and death.

Symbols serve as triggers of commitment in religions. They enshrine the teachings and express them in a tangible way. So the sacraments of baptism and the Lord's Supper in Christianity bring the believer into a practical relationship with otherwise abstract ideas, such as repentance and forgiveness. People can hardly live without symbols because they always need something to motivate life; it is as though abstract ideas need to be set within a symbol before individuals can be impelled to act upon them. When any attempt is made to turn symbols into bare statements of truth, this vital trigger of the emotions can easily be lost.

Douglas Davies

CHAPTER 4

The Sociology of Religion

The sociological study of religion has its roots in the seventeenth- and eighteenth-century Enlightenment, when a number of influential thinkers sought not only to question religious belief, but also to understand it as a natural phenomenon, a human product rather than the result of divine revelation or revealed truth. While contemporary sociology of religion has largely abandoned the overtly critical stance of early theoretical approaches to the truth claims of religion, the discipline retains the essential principle that an understanding of religion must acknowledge that it is, to some degree at least, socially constructed, and that social processes are fundamentally involved in the emergence, development, and dissemination of religious beliefs and practices.

METHODOLOGICAL AGNOSTICISM

While some sociologists consider that some religious beliefs are false, and that recognition of this is crucial to a sociological understanding of them, the dominant position in the sociology of religion today is that of 'methodological agnosticism'. This method states that it is neither possible, nor necessary, to decide whether beliefs are true or false in order to study them sociologically. Theology and philosophy of religion, not sociology, discuss questions of religious truth. The conditions which promote the acceptance or rejection of religious beliefs and practices, which govern their dissemination and the impact they have on behaviour and on society, can all be investigated without prior determination of their truth or falsity.

ROOTS IN INDIVIDUAL NEEDS

Theoretical approaches in the sociology of religion can usefully – if a little crudely – be divided into those which perceive the roots of religion to lie in individual needs and propensities, and those which perceive its roots to lie in social processes and to stem from the characteristics of society and social groups. The former may be further divided into those which emphasize cognitive processes – intellectualism – and those which emphasize various feelings and emotions – emotionalism.

In the nineteenth century, intellectualist theorists such as Auguste Comte (1798–1857), Edward Burnett Tylor (1832–1917), James G. Frazer (1854–1941), and Herbert Spencer (1820–1903) analyzed religious belief as essentially a pre-scientific attempt to understand the world and human experience, which would increasingly be supplanted by sound scientific knowledge. The future would thus be entirely secular, with no place for religion.

Emotionalist theorists, such as Robert Ranulph Marett (1866–1943), Bronislaw Malinowski (1884–1942), and Sigmund Freud (1856–1939), saw religions as stemming from human emotions such as fear, uncertainty, ambivalence, and awe. They were not attempts to explain and understand, but to cope with intense emotional experience.

ROOTS IN SOCIAL PROCESSES

The most influential sociological approaches that consider the roots of religion lie in society and social processes, not in the individual, are those of Karl Marx (1818–83) and Émile Durkheim (1858–1917).

For Marx, religion was both a form of ideology supported by ruling classes in order to control the masses, and at the same time an expression of protest against such oppression – 'the sigh of the oppressed creature'. As a protest, however, it changed nothing, promoting only resignation, and promising resolution of problems in the afterlife. Religion is 'the opium of the people', in the sense that it dulls the pain of the oppressed and thereby stops them from revolting. Hence, the oppressed turn to religion to help them get through life; the ruling classes promote it to keep them in check. It will simply disappear when the social conditions that cause it are removed.

> Religion is the sigh of the oppressed creature and the opium of the people.
>
> Karl Marx, *A Contribution to the Critique of Hegel's Philosophy of Right* (Deutsch-Französische Jahrbücher, 1844).

Durkheim saw religion as an essential, integrating social force, which fulfilled basic functions in society. It was the expression of human subordination, not to a ruling class, as Marx had argued, but rather to the requirements of society itself, and to social pressures which overrule individual preferences. In his famous work *The Elementary Forms of the Religious Life* (1912), Durkheim argued that 'Religion is society worshipping itself.' God may not exist, but society does; rather than God exerting pressure on the individual to conform, society itself exerts the pressure. Individuals, who do not understand the nature of society and social groups, use the language of religion to explain the social forces they experience. Although people misinterpret social forces as religious forces, what they experience is real. Moreover, for Durkheim, religion fulfils a positive role, in that it binds society together as a moral community.

MAX WEBER AND MEANING THEORY

Later theoretical approaches in the sociology of religion have all drawn extensively on this earlier work, attempting to synthesize its insights into more nuanced approaches, in which the various strands of intellectual, emotional, and social factors are woven together. A notable example is the work of Max Weber (1864–1920), probably the most significant contributor to the sociology of religion to this day. His work included one of the best-known treatises in the sub-discipline, *The Protestant Ethic and the Spirit of Capitalism* (1904–05), and three major studies of world religions.

Weber's approach to religion was the forerunner of what has become known as 'meaning theory', which emphasizes the way in which religion gives meaning to human life and society, in the face of apparently arbitrary suffering and injustice. Religion offers explanation and justification of good and of bad fortune, by locating them within a broader picture of a reality which may go beyond the world of immediate everyday perception, thereby helping to make sense of what always threatens to appear senseless. So those who suffer undeservedly in this life may have offended in a previous one; or they will receive their just deserts in the next life, or in heaven. Those who prosper through wickedness will ultimately be judged and duly punished.

RATIONAL CHOICE THEORY

The most recent, general theoretical approach in the sociology of religion, which synthesizes many previous insights, is that of 'rational choice theory'. Drawing upon economic theory, this treats religions as rival products offered in a market by religious organizations – which are compared to commercial firms – and leaders, to consumers, who choose by assessing which best meets their needs, which is most reliable, and so on. This approach promises to provide many insights. However, it has been subjected to trenchant criticism by those who question whether religion can be treated as something chosen in the way that products such as cars or soap-powders are chosen, rather than something into which people are socialized, and which forms an important part of their identity that cannot easily be set aside or changed. Furthermore, if religious beliefs are a matter of preference and convenience, why do their followers accept the uncongenial demands and constraints they usually impose, and the threat of punishments for failure to comply?

SECULARIZATION AND NEW MOVEMENTS

The sociology of religion was for many decades regarded as an insignificant branch of sociology. This situation has changed in recent years, especially in the USA. Substantive empirical inquiry has been dominated by two areas: secularization and religious sects, cults, and movements. It had been widely assumed that religion was declining in modern industrial societies and losing its social significance – the secularization thesis. This has

been questioned and found by many — especially rational choice theorists — to be wanting. The result has been intense

Hare Krishna Festival of Chariots in Trafalgar Square, London. Hare Krishna is one of many New Religious Movements.

debate. The dominant position now, though not unchallenged, is that the secularization thesis was a myth.

Central to this debate is the claim that — while religion in its traditional forms may be declining in some modern, Western industrial societies — it is not declining in all of them, the USA being a notable exception; and that novel forms of religion are continuously emerging to meet inherent spiritual needs. Some new forms are clearly religious in character. Others, it is claimed, are quite unlike religion as commonly understood, and include alternative and complementary forms of healing, psychotherapies, techniques for the development of human potential, deep ecology, holistic spirituality, New Age, the cult of celebrity, nationalist movements, and even sport. Whether such things can be considered forms of religion depends upon how religion is defined, a matter much disputed.

A second crucial element in the secularization debate is the rise of a diversity of sects and cults – the New Religious Movements – which have proliferated since the 1960s and 1970s. For the anti-secularization – or 'sacralization' – theorists, this flourishing of novel religiosity gives the lie to the thesis; while for pro-secularization theorists, such movements fall far short of making up for the decline of mainstream churches and denominations. Whatever their significance for the secularization thesis, the New Religious Movements – and sects and cults in general – have fascinated sociologists, whose extensive studies of them form a major part of the subject.

Heavy concentration on New Religious Movements has been balanced more recently by studies of more mainstream religious churches and communities, and by studies of the religious life of ethnic minorities and immigrant communities, among whom religion is often particularly significant and an important element of identity. Added to the interest in new forms of religion and quasi-religion, such studies make the contemporary sociology of religion more diverse and varied than ever.

MALCOLM HAMILTON

CHAPTER 5

The Psychology of Religion

Three key figures dominate the psychology of religion that we have inherited from the pre-World War II period: William James, Sigmund Freud, and C. G. Jung.

WILLIAM JAMES (1842–1910)

The undoubted masterpiece of the early days of the psychology of religion is the classic *Varieties of Religious Experience*, written by William James at the end of the nineteenth century. James assembled an interesting compendium of personal reports of religious experience, and embedded them in a rich and subtle framework of analysis. He thought religious experience was essentially an individual matter, the foundation on which religious doctrine and church life were built. However, from the outset his critics argued that religious experience is in fact interpreted within the framework of inherited religious teaching and shaped by the life of the institution. James hoped to put religion on a scientific basis, through the scientific study of religious experience, although he was unable to make a really convincing case for accepting religious experience at face value. Despite these issues, even his critics have never doubted the quality of his work, which is as hotly debated now as when it was first written.

SIGMUND FREUD (1856–1939)

Another important figure in the development of the psychology of religion was Sigmund Freud, although his approach was very different from that of James. Freud built his general theories upon what patients told him during their psychoanalysis, although he reported only one case study in which religion played a central part. This was the so-called 'wolf man', in whom religion and obsessionality were intertwined, which led Freud to suggest that religion was a universal form of obsessional neurosis. In fact, Freud's psychology of religion was hardly based on data at all; it was a blend of general psychoanalytic theory and his own personal hostility to religion. He wrote several books about religion, each taking a different approach. The clearest is *The Future of an Illusion*, which claims that religion is merely 'illusion', which for him is a technical term meaning wish-fulfilment.

Freud's successors have argued that what he called illusion, including religion, is in fact much more valuable than he realized to people in helping them to adjust to life.

C. G. JUNG (1875–1961)

Freud's approach to religion was continued in modified form by Carl Gustav Jung. Whereas Freud had been a harsh critic of religion, Jung was favourably disposed to it. However, his approach to religion was so idiosyncratic that many have found him an uncomfortable friend. Jung made a distinction between the ego – the centre of conscious life – and the self – the whole personality that people can potentially become. For Jung, the self is the image of God in the psyche, and the process of 'individuation' – that is, development from

Sigmund Freud (1856–1939).

ego-centred life to self-centred life – is in some ways analogous to religious salvation. Jung was evasive about the question of whether there was a god beyond the psyche, and usually said it was not a question for him as a psychologist. Jung took more interest in the significance of Christian doctrine than most psychologists and, for example, wrote long essays on the Mass and on the Trinity.

> Religious ideas … are illusions, fulfilments of the oldest, strongest, and most urgent wishes of mankind.
>
> Sigmund Freud, *The Future of an Illusion* (London: Hogarth, 1962).

THE PSYCHOLOGY OF RELIGION TODAY

The psychology of religion went relatively quiet around the middle of the twentieth century, but has been reviving in recent decades. It has become more explicitly scientific, and most psychological research on religion now uses quantitative methods. There are currently no big psychological theories of religion, but important insights have been obtained about various specific aspects of religion. The following examples give a flavour of current work.

- *Individual differences.* One useful distinction has been between 'intrinsic' religious people – those for whom religion is the dominant motivation in their lives – and 'extrinsic' religious people – those for whom religion meets other needs. Intrinsics and extrinsics differ from one another in many ways. For example, it has been suggested that intrinsically religious people show less social prejudice than non-religious people, whereas extrinsically religious people show more.

- *Religious development.* Children's understanding of religion follows a predictable path, moving from the concrete to the abstract. However, acquiring a better intellectual understanding of religion is not necessarily accompanied by a more spiritual experience. In fact, spiritual experience may actually decline as children grow up. There have been attempts to extend a development approach to religion into adulthood. For example, James Fowler developed a general theory of 'faith development'. Although this has identified different approaches to faith in adults, it is not clear that higher levels of faith necessarily follow the earlier ones, nor that they are superior.
- *Mental health.* Despite Freud's view that religion is a form of neurosis, scientific research has shown that there is often a positive correlation between religion and health, especially mental health. It is most likely that religion actually helps to improve people's mental health, although this is hard to prove conclusively. Religion probably helps by providing a framework of meaning and a supportive community, both of which enable people to cope better with stressful experiences.
- *Conservative and charismatic Christianity.* There has been much interest in both fundamentalism and charismatic religion. One key feature of fundamentalism is the 'black and white' mindset that maintains a sharp dichotomy between truth and falsehood, and between insiders and outsiders. The charismatic phenomenon that has attracted most research interest is speaking in tongues. It seems very unlikely that this is an actual language; it is probably more a form of ecstatic utterance. One line of research has explored the social context in which people learn to speak in tongues, and another the unusual state of consciousness in which people surrender voluntary control of their speech.

Although psychology has generally taken a detached, scientific view of religion, there are other points of contact. One is the incorporation of psychological methods into the Christian church's pastoral care, begun by Freud's Lutheran pastor friend, Oskar Pfister (1873–1956). Another is the dialogue between religious and psychological world-views, an aspect of the more general dialogue between science and religion. Some psychologists consider that humans are 'nothing but' the product of their evolution or their nervous systems, whereas religious faith emphasizes their importance in the purposes of God.

FRASER WATTS

CHAPTER 6

Theological Approaches to the Study of Religion

During the development of the study of religion as a new discipline in the twentieth century, the pioneers of the field were often at pains to stress that what they did was different from theology. As such, it might be asked whether a theological approach even belongs within the study of religion. Many scholars today, who emphasize it as a scientific or historical discipline, distance themselves from any notion that theology, in any form, has a place within the study of religion. For others, the relationship is more ambiguous, while some scholars even argue that theological approaches are essential to understanding, and so truly studying, religion.

WHAT DO WE MEAN BY 'THEOLOGY'?

It is best to start by defining what we mean by 'theology' in relation to the study of religion. We will begin with some negatives. First, it does not mean a confessional approach, where the teachings of one school, tradition, or sect within a religion are taught as the true, or correct, understanding of that religion. Second, theology does not imply that there is any need for a belief, or faith content, within the person studying in that idiom. It is not, therefore, under the classic definition of the medieval Christian Anselm of Canterbury (1033–1109), an act of 'faith seeking understanding'.

We come now to the positives. First, it is about understanding the internal terms within which a religion will seek to explain itself, its teachings, and its formulations. We must be clear here that 'theology' is used loosely, because while it makes sense as a Christian term — literally it is the study of God — and can be fairly clearly applied to other theistic traditions, it is also used elsewhere to talk about broadly philosophical traditions related to transcendence. Accordingly, people use the term 'Buddhist theology' — although others question whether this usage is appropriate, but space does not permit us to engage in such disputes here. Second, it means engaging with empathy with questions of meaning as they would make sense within the religious worldview, and so goes beyond reasoning and relates to a way of life. Here, we see clear resonances with phenomenological approaches, where we seek to understand a religion on its own terms.

Indeed, without a theological viewpoint, it can be argued   Anselm of Canterbury (1033–1109).
that the study of religions fails, because on the one hand it is
either simply reductionist, that is to say it explains via some chosen system why the religion
exists, what it does, and what it means – as tends to be the case with some parts of the
sociology or psychology of religion. Or, on the other hand, it becomes merely descriptive,
telling us what rituals are performed, what the ethics are, what the teachings are, how it is
lived out, and so on – a simply phenomenological approach. A theological approach looks
into the religion, and seeks to understand what it means to believers within its own terms,
and how that system works as a rational worldview to those within it.

INSIDER AND OUTSIDER

Two important pairs of distinctions are useful to consider how theological approaches are applied. The first, developed by the anthropologist Kenneth Pike (1912–2000), and often applied to religion, concerns what are called 'emic' and 'etic' approaches. An emic approach attempts to explain things within the cultural world of the believer. An etic approach is the way an external observer would try and make sense of the behaviours and beliefs of a society or group in some form of scientific sense. Within anthropology, these basic distinctions are seen as part of the tools of the trade. Unless she enters into the thought-world of a group, culture, and society, the anthropologist will remain forever exterior, and will not understand what things mean to those in that group. Moreover, emic understandings can help inspire etic description, and assess its appropriateness. Clearly, in the study of religion, this originally anthropological distinction suggests that an emic, or theological, approach is justified.

Our second pair of distinctions is the notion of 'Insider' and 'Outsider' perspectives. These are, respectively, concepts from somebody who is a believer (an Insider), and a non-believer, that is, the scholar (an Outsider). This differs from the emic/etic distinction, because they are always perspectives of the Outsider: the scholar. As such, an emic theological approach is different from the confessional theology of an Insider. However, this distinction is often blurred. Field anthropologists speak of spending so much time within the group or society they study that they often almost become part of that group, and part of good fieldwork is about entering the life world of those studied. This applies equally to scholars of religion, especially those engaged in fieldwork.

Another issue is that scholars may be believers within a religion, and so may inhabit both Insider and Outsider worlds. This raises many interesting questions, but here we will note simply that the notion of the detached, impartial, and objective scholar is increasingly questioned. Issues raised by critical theory have suggested that every standpoint will always have a bias, and some have argued further – notably the Hindu scholar, Gavin Flood – that a religious point of view, if openly acknowledged, can form part of the broader study of religions. Moreover, religious groups are often affected by what scholars of religion say about them. Therefore, Insider worldviews and Outsider descriptions – etic or emic – become intertwined in a dance that affects each other. As such, the question of how a theological approach fits into, or works within, religious studies is far from simple.

ALWAYS 'TAINTED'?

Scholars such as Timothy Fitzgerald, Tomoko Masuzawa, and Tala Asad have argued that the supposedly secular study of religion has always been 'tainted', because it developed in a world where Christianity dominated – often with a particular kind of liberal theology – so that no study of religion is entirely free from theology. Certainly, some foundational figures, such as Mircea Eliade, had a religious worldview, and a lot of mid-twentieth century work developing the phenomenology of religion, or comparative religion, made assumptions about a religious realm that underlay all traditions. However, it is arguable whether all scholars of religion then and since are affected in this way, while a case can be made that it was not solely Christian assumptions that affected the study of religion, but that such assumptions were shaped by the encounter with various religious traditions. As such, while we must be suspicious of some categories within the study of religion, we do not need to assume that everything has a Christian basis. Indeed, Frank Whaling argues we must also not forget that many religions have a lot to say about other religions, and this leads into theorizing on comparative religion, comparative theology, and the theology of religions within a confessional standpoint which is not entirely separate from understanding a religion and its worldview.

The relationship of the study of religions and theology varies in different countries. For instance, in Germany the two tend to be starkly polarized, with theology departments being – at least traditionally – strictly confessional, normally Roman Catholic or Protestant, and the study of religions – understood as a primarily reductionist secular discipline – is always separate from theology. In the UK, the ancient universities started to admit non-Anglican Christian denominations from the nineteenth century, and so lost their confessional stance, with seminaries for training priests becoming separate or linked institutions. For this reason, it was easier to start teaching theology from a generic standpoint, which could integrate other religions as part of the curriculum, and so there are many combined departments for theology and the study of religion. The USA tends to have a more separate system, although there are places where an active study of religion discipline exists within a theology department. Obviously, such regional differences affect the way a theological approach to the study of religion is accepted or understood.

PAUL HEDGES

CHAPTER 7

Critical Theory and Religion

Our knowledge of 'religion' is always politically shaped, and never an innocent or a neutral activity. Knowledge about religion can always be questioned, and scholars of religion are finding that 'religion', and talk about 'religion', is involved with questions of power. Critical theory questions knowledge about 'religion', and reveals the social and political nature of such ideas.

DEFINING CRITICAL THEORY

Critical theory arises from a long tradition in Western thought which has questioned the truth and certainty of knowledge. It carries forward the work of the 'three great masters of suspicion', Karl Marx (1818–83), Friedrich Nietzsche (1844–1900), and Sigmund Freud (1856–1939). Following Marx, critical theory is aware that all knowledge is linked to economic and political ideology; following Nietzsche, it understands that all knowledge is linked to the 'will to power'; and following Freud, it understands that all knowledge is linked to things outside our awareness (the unconscious). The ideas of these three great thinkers influence, and are carried forward in, the work of critical theory. All three started to question the view that knowledge was neutral and rational.

Friedrich Nietzsche (1844–1900).

There are two basic understandings of 'critical theory', a strict definition and a loose definition. The former relates to the Frankfurt School of Critical Theory, an important group of German intellectuals who tried to think about society according to the ideas of Marx and Freud.

They included Theodor Adorno (1903–69) and Max Horkheimer (1895–1973), who jointly published *Dialectic of Enlightenment*, a seminal work in which they questioned Western rational thought since the Enlightenment. What did it say about the potential of human knowledge if it could lead to the ideology of Nazi Germany and the horrors of the Holocaust? Culture was understood to be formed by propagandist manipulation.

The loose definition incorporates a wider range of critical theories, which emerged – largely in France – after the student riots of 1968 in Paris. This date is a watershed in modern Western intellectual history because it reflects, among many things, a shift in the thinking about state power and the control of ideas. It was an event that brought the questions of 'power' and 'politics' to the question of knowledge and truth.

POST-STRUCTURALISM

The critical thinking that emerged in 1968 in France is known as 'post-structuralism' because it comes after an intellectual movement known as 'structuralism'. Structuralism held that one could identify a given number of structures in myth, language, and the world. Post-structuralists argued that these structures were not 'given' in the fabric of the world, but created by different societies at different points of history and in different cultures. Michel Foucault (1926–84) examined the historical nature of ideas, showing that the ways we think about the world are related to political institutions and regimes of power. Jacques Derrida (1930–2004) showed that our ways of representing the world in texts holds hidden contradictions and tensions, because language is unstable and built upon assertions of power, not truth. The instability of language refers to the discovery that the meaning of words in a dictionary simply means other words, rather than something indisputable and fixed in the world, and that meanings are simply asserted or agreed, rather than having a strong foundation given for all time. These two prominent thinkers brought knowledge under question, and enabled scholars of religion to uncover how what is and what is not classified as 'religion' can benefit certain groups of people within society.

Critical theory is thus not an abstract and disengaged way of thinking, but an active ethical responsibility for the world and the way we think about the world. It shows the link between ideas and political practices.

> *Religion is a political force.*
>
> Michel Foucault

THE END OF PHENOMENOLOGY

Before critical theory, the study of religion often consisted of representing different religious traditions, and understanding them according to their rituals, beliefs, and practices. This is known as 'the phenomenology of religion', and is arguably still dominant in school and university programmes of study. Such an approach assumed that knowledge is neutral, and that different issues can be presented without too much difficulty. It was also assumed by many scholars that one does not need a 'theory' or 'theoretical position' –

a way of understanding knowledge and the world – to represent a religious tradition or a set of ideas. There was an assumption that language neutrally represented the external world according to a direct correspondence between the subject in representation (words) and the object in the external world (things) – in this case 'religious' things. However, knowledge and the categories used to represent the world and religion are now seen to be carrying hidden assumptions, with implications for gender, society, politics, colonial history, race, and ethnicity. All knowledge is now seen as reflecting a particular viewpoint or bias about the world; the production and acquisition of knowledge is never neutral. Hence, after critical theory, there is no neutral presentation of ideas about religion.

Critical theory is a way of thinking about how our dominant conceptions of religion come to be dominant or hegemonic. It seeks to identify the hidden positions within our knowledge, and to recognize that all ideas about religion hold a theoretical position about knowledge, even if that position is denied or not apparent. Critical theory offers a way of exploring 'religion' through a set of critical questions about the world and the ideas under discussion. It is not limited to the study of religion, but applies to all ways of thinking about the world, and even questions the boundary between different disciplines of knowledge. Critical theory is not a sub-discipline of religious studies – like the sociology, anthropology, or psychology of religion – but cuts across all these areas and questions all types of knowledge.

Critical theory questions the very idea of 'religion' as a Western – even Christian – category that assumes that belief is more important than how people live, which in turn is used to make assumptions about what people outside Christianity believe. This is seen as a distortion of other cultures. To correct such a view, critical theory considers traditions and cultures outside the bias of such an idea, which assumes there is something special and distinctive we can call 'religion' or 'religious'. For example, scholars question the Christian missionary interpretation of other cultures, and ask whether Hinduism is a 'religion' or the culture of South Asia. In turn, we may question whether Western capitalism is a culture or a religion. Critical theory draws attention to how knowledge is related to political ideas, and questions the domination of Western ideas (particularly European-American ideas) over other ways of seeing the world in different cultures and periods of history. It explores the way ideas powerfully rule the world and the 'truth' people have about the world.

RELIGION, POWER, AND CULTURE

Critical theory shows that the ways we think about religion are bound up in questions of power. Religious studies is now involved in exploring how the history and abuses of colonialism influenced the emergence of religion as an idea; how state power, political regimes, and the globalized world of capitalism affect this process; and how the mass media alter what we mean by religion, and uncover those activities and groups within society not recognized as religious. Critical theory exposes the abuses of power in history, and examines who benefits from thinking about the world in certain ways. It identifies those who are marginalized and unable to speak for themselves.

By examining race, gender, sexuality, and economic wealth one can see how ideas about religion often support those in power, usually the ruling educated elite of white, Western men. Thinking and writing about ideas from the position of the exploited radically changes the subject and the writing of history. Such a process questions, for example, the narrative of Christian history from its Roman-European bias, and examines Christianity through its African – particularly Ethiopian – traditions, highlighting the importance of Augustine as an African. It explores the involvement of Buddhist monks in political activism, and uncovers how the Western media distort the understanding of Islam. Critical theory also identifies ways of life outside the mainstream traditions, and explores the indigenous or local traditions around the world, which are suppressed by multinational business interests for land and oil.

Orthodox priests at a Christian festival at Timket, Ethiopia.

Critical theory questions the boundary between religion and culture, and argues that what people do – rather than what they believe – is more important in understanding. The distinction between the religious and the secular is seen as an ideological or political tool. According to this view, the category of 'religion' can be applied to all cultural activities, such as football, shopping, fashion, club-culture, and film. The historical roots of social institutions – such as government, schools, hospitals, and law – are shown to carry ideas that can be classified as religious, even if they are not transparent. Critical theory radically alters the understanding of religion and shows the importance of the idea to world history. After critical theory, the study of religion becomes a political activity, an account of how powerful organizations in different parts of the world shape the way we understand and classify the world.

JEREMY CARRETTE

CHAPTER 8

Ritual and Performance

Like myths and symbols, ritual and performance is an area that has particularly interested religious studies scholars. Ritual is patterned, formal, symbolic action. Religious ritual is usually seen as having reference to divine or transcendent beings, or perhaps ancestors, whom the participants invoke, propitiate, feed – through offering or sacrifice – worship, or otherwise communicate with. Rituals attempt to enact and deal with the central dilemmas of human existence: continuity and stability, growth and fertility, morality and immortality or transcendence. They have the potential to transform people and situations, creating a fierce warrior or docile wife, a loving servant or imperious tyrant. The ambiguity of ritual symbols, and the invocation of supernatural power, magnifies and disguises human needs and emotions. Because rituals are sometimes performed in terrifying circumstances – as in certain initiation rituals – the messages they carry act at a psycho-biological level that includes, but also exceeds, the rational mind. Symbols and sacred objects are manipulated within ritual to enhance performance and communicate ideological messages concerning the nature of the individual, society, and cosmos. Rituals are fundamental to human culture, and can be used to control, subvert, stabilize, enhance, or terrorize individuals and groups. Studying them gives us a key to an understanding and interpretation of culture.

Anthropologists and religious studies scholars sometimes look at rituals in terms of what they do. For instance, Catherine Bell (b. 1953) distinguishes between:
- rites of passage or 'life crisis' rituals
- calendrical rituals and commemorative rites
- rites of exchange or communication
- rites of affliction
- rites of feasting, fasting, festivals
- political rituals

Another approach is to focus on their explanatory value. Mircea Eliade (1907–86) was interested in ritual as a re-enactment of a primal, cosmogonic myth, bringing the past continually into the present. Robin Horton emphasizes the reality of the religious beliefs behind ritual actions. Using the Kalabari of Nigeria as an example, he insists that religious rituals have the power to move and transform participants because they express beliefs that have meaning and coherence for their adherents. Taking a lead from Durkheim (1858–1917), other scholars claim that rituals are effective because they make statements about social phenomena. Maurice Bloch, writing about circumcision rituals in Madagascar, makes the interesting observation that because a ritual is not fully a statement and not fully an action it allows its message to be simultaneously communicated and disguised. In some cases ritual symbols may be full of resonance, as Victor Turner demonstrated for Ndembu heali ng, chiefly installation, and initiation rituals in Central Africa. In other cases the performance of the ritual itself may be what matters, the content or symbolism having become redundant or forgotten over time, as Fritz Staal has argued for Vedic rituals in India.

> *No experience is too lowly to be taken up in ritual and given a lofty meaning.*
>
> Mary Douglas

PATTERNS IN RITUAL

A key figure in the study of ritual is Arnold van Gennep (1873–1957), who discerned an underlying patterning beneath a wide range of rituals. Whether we look at seasonal festivals such as Christmas, midsummer, or harvest, or 'life crisis' rituals that mark a change in status from one stage of life to another, such as birth, puberty, marriage, or mortuary rituals, we see beneath them all the threefold pattern of separation, transition, and reintegration. Van Gennep also noted that there is generally a physical passage in ritual as well as a social movement, and that the first time a ritual is celebrated it is usually more elaborate than on subsequent occasions, as it bears the weight of change of status.

Victor Turner took up van Gennep's schema, emphasizing the movement from social structure to an anti-structural position in the middle, liminal, stage of a rite of passage. In the middle stage, initiands often share certain characteristics. There is a levelling process — they may be stripped, or dressed in such a way as to erase individuality, hair may be shaved or allowed to grow long. Neophytes are often isolated from the everyday world, and may undergo certain ordeals that bind them to one another and to those initiating them. Turner coined the term 'communitas' to describe a spontaneous, immediate, and concrete relatedness that is typical of people in the liminal stage of a rite of passage. Liminality can also be institutionalized and extended almost indefinitely, as for instance in the military, monastic communities, hospitals, or asylums.

MALE AND FEMALE INITIATION

Bruce Lincoln has criticized both van Gennep and Turner's models as more relevant to male than female initiations, pointing out that women have little status in the social hierarchy, and therefore the middle stage of a woman's initiation is less likely to stress anti-structural elements. Rather than being brought low as a prelude to being elevated, her lowlier place within society is reinforced. A woman is more likely than her male counterparts to be initiated singly, and to be enclosed within a domestic space. Women are generally adorned rather than stripped, and the nature of the knowledge

Malagasy children, Madagascar.

passed on during initiation is likely to be mundane rather than esoteric. Rather than separation, liminality, and reintegration, Lincoln proposes that for women initiation is more likely to involve enclosure, metamorphosis or magnification, and emergence.

A ritual is a type of performance, but not all performances are rituals. Richard Schechner (b. 1934) has pointed out that whether a performance is to be classified as ritual or theatre depends on the context. If the purpose of a performance is to be efficacious, it is a ritual. If its purpose is to entertain, it is theatre. These are not absolute distinctions, and most performances contain elements of both efficacious intention and entertainment. At the ritual end of the continuum we are likely to have an active 'audience', who share the aims and intentions of the main actors. Time and space are sacred, and symbolically marked, and it is the end result of the action that matters — to heal, initiate, aid the deceased, or whatever it may be. In a theatrical performance, the audience is more likely to observe than participate, and the event is an end in itself. It is performed for those watching, and not for, or in the presence of, a higher power or absent other.

FIONA BOWIE

QUESTIONS

1. What is a religion, and why can the term be problematic?

2. Why did many phenomenologists reject theological approaches to religion?

3. An atheist will always be a more objective student of religion than a believer. How far do you agree or disagree with this statement?

4. What problems might you encounter in studying a religion as an outsider?

5. What did Marx mean when he referred to religion as 'the sigh of the oppressed creature'?

6. How do Marx and Weber differ in their perceptions of religion?

7. Explain Durkheim's view of the role of religion in society.

8. Why has there been renewed interest in the sociology of religion in recent years?

9. What can psychology tell us about why people may hold religious beliefs?

10. How has Critical Theory influenced our understanding of religion since the 1960s?

FURTHER READING

Connolly, Peter (ed.), *Approaches to the Study of Religion*. London: Continuum, 2001.

Eliade, Mircea, *The Sacred and the Profane: The Nature of Religion*. New York: Harcourt, Brace, 1959.

Fitzgerald, Timothy, *The Ideology of Religious Studies*. Oxford: Oxford University Press, 2000.

Flood, Gavin, *Beyond Phenomenology: Rethinking the Study of Religion*. London: Cassell, 1999.

Geertz, Clifford, 'Religion as a Cultural System', in Michael Banton, ed., *Anthropological Approaches to the Study of Religion*, pp. 1–46. London: Tavistock, 1966.

Kunin, Seth D., *Religion: The Modern Theories*. Baltimore: Johns Hopkins University Press, 2003.

Levi-Strauss, Claude, *Myth and Meaning*. Toronto: University of Toronto Press, 1978.

McCutcheon, Russell T. ed., *The Insider/Outsider Problem in the Study of Religion*. London: Cassell, 1999.

Otto, Rudolf, *The Idea of the Holy*. London: Oxford University Press, 1923.

Pals, Daniel L., *Eight Theories of Religion*. New York: Oxford University Press, 2006.

Van der Leeuw, Gerardus, *Religion in Essence and Manifestation*. London: Allen & Unwin, 1938.

TIMELINE OF WORLD RELIGIONS

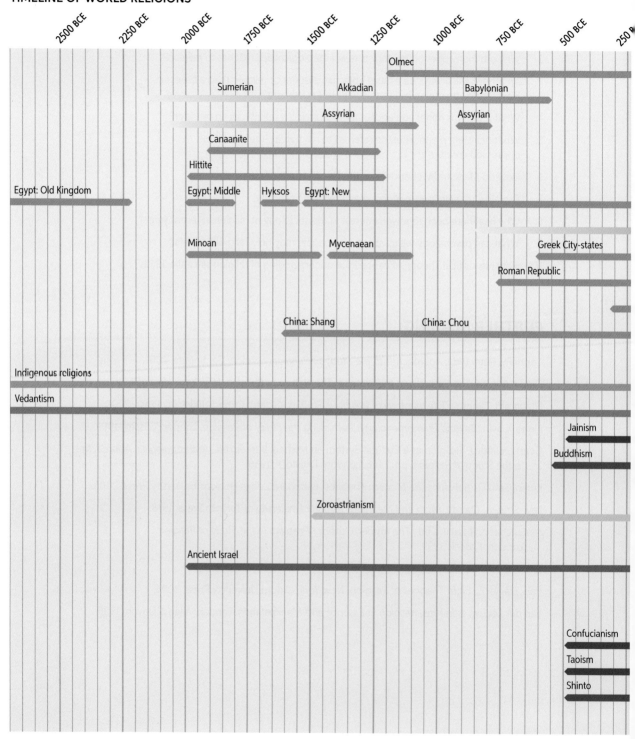

A BRIEF INTRODUCTION TO BUDDHISM

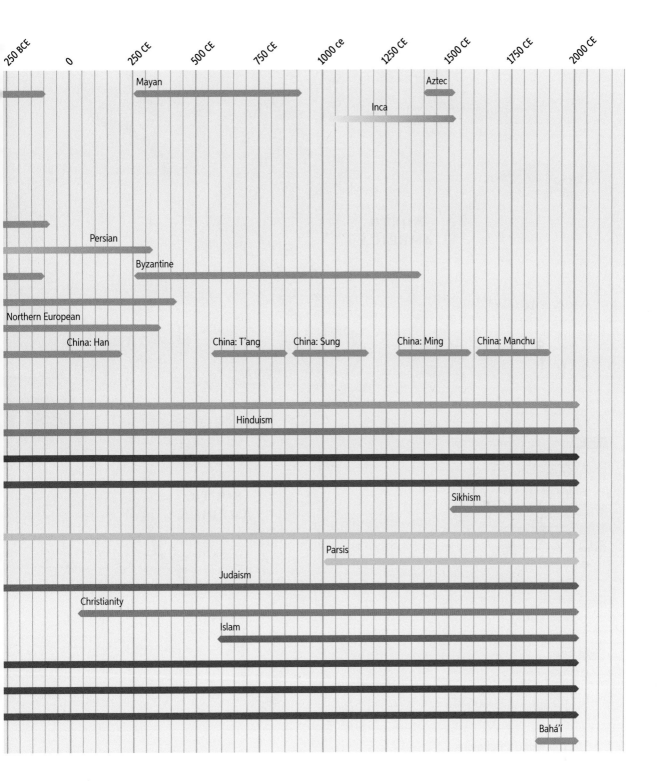

250 BCE   0   250 CE   500 CE   750 CE   1000 ce   1250 CE   1500 CE   1750 CE   2000 CE

Mayan

Aztec

Inca

Persian

Byzantine

Northern European

China: Han   China: T'ang   China: Sung   China: Ming   China: Manchu

Hinduism

Sikhism

Parsis

Judaism

Christianity

Islam

Bahá'í

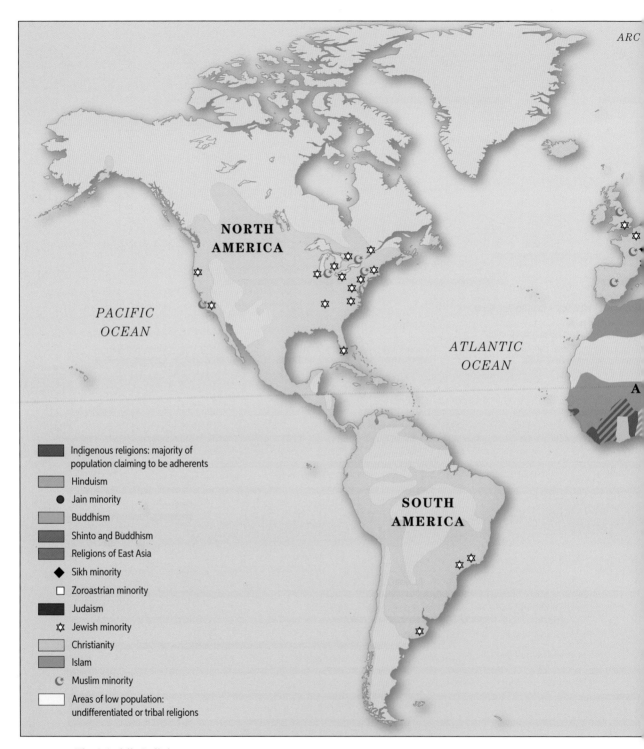

The World's Religions

ATLANTIC
OCEAN

PACIFIC
OCEAN

NORTH
AMERICA

SOUTH
AMERICA

Legend:

- Indigenous religions: majority of population claiming to be adherents
- Hinduism
- ● Jain minority
- Buddhism
- Shinto and Buddhism
- Religions of East Asia
- ◆ Sikh minority
- ☐ Zoroastrian minority
- Judaism
- ✡ Jewish minority
- Christianity
- Islam
- ☪ Muslim minority
- Areas of low population: undifferentiated or tribal religions

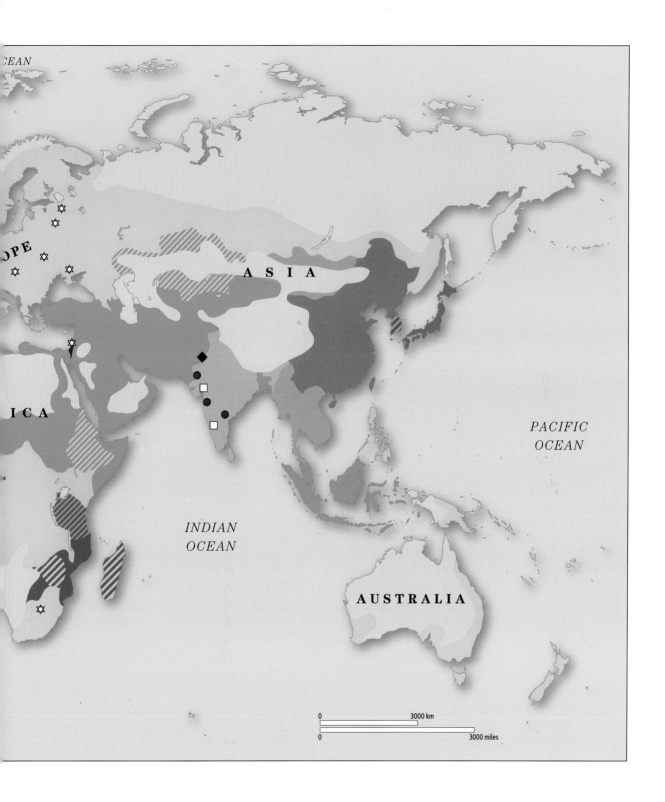

PART 2
BUDDHISM

SUMMARY

Buddhism, it is now generally believed, emerged into the world sometime around the fifth century BCE, in northern India, and is derived from the teachings of one man – Siddhartha Gautama – known to his followers by the title Buddha. Central to the Buddha's teachings was the idea that one had to experience dissatisfaction or suffering in order to understand that these have a cause: the egocentric desire for satisfaction, pleasure, or even life itself. Once this understanding is reached, followers of the *Dharma*, 'the teaching', can begin their quest for enlightenment, *nirvana*, by following the Buddhist moral code, and by meditating in order to purify the mind. As a non-theistic religion, Buddhism does not concern itself with the existence of a creator, in the Western sense at least, teaching that attainment of *nirvana* is a person's route out of the endless cycle of death and rebirth.

A variety of different schools and monastic traditions emerged within Buddhism, from *Theravada*, the earliest surviving monastic school, to *Tantra*, which advocates the use of ritual magic to control hidden forces or aid the path to *nirvana*. One of the most important traditions is *Mahayana*, through which some seek not only to achieve *nirvana* but actually to become a Buddha. Regional variations also emerged, as Buddhism spread outward from India across much of eastern Asia. In many cases, these variations are closely related to local religious traditions, or are even the product of wider syncretism, such as the Cao Dai in Vietnam, which has roots not only in Buddhism but also Catholic Christianity, Confucianism, and Taoism. In recent decades, Buddhism has faced suppression in many Asian countries, perhaps most notably in Tibet, where rule by Maoist China led to severe repression of the local traditions. Alongside this, though, Buddhism has experienced growth elsewhere, buoyed both by migration and Western interest in the religion.

CHAPTER 9

A Historical Overview

Buddhism is the '-ism' that is named after the Buddha. 'Buddha' is not a personal name, but a title meaning 'the one who has awakened'. The Buddha was a historical individual who lived and died some centuries BCE, although it is difficult to be precise about his exact dates. The common traditional date for the Buddha's birth is 563 BCE, and the sources agree he lived in North India for eighty years. However, modern scholarship questions the reliability of this date, and most historians place his birth eighty to a hundred years later, and his death around 400 BCE. The Buddha's clan-name was Gautama, but later tradition called him Siddhartha in Sanskrit, or Siddhattha in the Pali language, in which many early Buddhist works were written.

'Buddhism' is an English name for a religion that its followers often simply refer to as the *Dharma* (Pali, *Dhamma*), which can be taken here as meaning both 'the teaching' and 'the way things are'. It was discovering this, and teaching it, that made Siddhartha Gautama 'the Buddha'. Whereas Western discussions tend to stress the importance of its founder (Buddha + ism, no doubt on the model of Christ + ianity), Buddhists prefer to emphasize not him, but rather what he taught; for them the obvious place to start is the teaching. This teaching, they say, leads people to understand how things truly are, and thence to a radical reassessment of their lives. The Buddha simply awakened to this truth and taught it. In this he was not unique, for — it is said — others had awakened before him, and there will be many, many after him too.

> *Hatred is never quenched by hatred; by non-hatred alone is hatred quenched. This is an Eternal Law.*
>
> *Dhammapada*, v. 5

WHO WAS THE BUDDHA?

To start with the life story of the Buddha is the Western tradition. Even if we start with it here too, this life story should not be read as historical fact, though we can reasonably take it that Siddhartha Gautama lived and died. He was considered by his followers to have achieved the fullest possible understanding of reality, an understanding that is true freedom. The historicity of the rest is difficult to assess. Some of it we know is very unlikely to have happened, but Buddhism has always been more interested in the ways in which the life story illustrates Buddhist teachings than in its literal historical truth.

The legendary account of the Buddha's life developed gradually in the centuries after his demise. In that account, he is a prince who is protected from all knowledge of the nasty things of life. However, in the Pali sources he is simply a highborn Shakyan who had little awareness of suffering as he grew up, but the shock of discovering old age, sickness, and death led him to renounce worldly pursuits. He had married and had a son, but left his family and took to the life – not uncommon in India then as now – of a wandering seeker. He sought the final truth that would lead to complete freedom from suffering – a harsh life of meditation, study, and asceticism. Food – and very little of it – came from asking for alms. But eventually Siddhartha, looking within, in deep meditation, reached the truth he sought. He came to 'see it the way it really is', and this truth set him free. He was now the awakened one, the Buddha. The Buddha gathered around him a group of disciples and wandered northern India, teaching all who would listen. Eventually, in old age, the Buddha died. But for him death was nothing; for he was now free from death, as he was free from all other forms of unpleasantness, imperfection, and frustration. After death, there is nothing more to say.

Chinese Buddha figurine.

WHAT DID HE TEACH?

The life story of the Buddha is all about things appearing one way and really being another. The Buddha taught that 'seeing things the way they really are' is the way to overcome every sort of unpleasantness, imperfection, and frustration. These are all classed under the expression *dukkha* (Pali), a term which in the everyday context of the time meant literally 'pain' or 'suffering'. He taught that, when we look deeply, we can see that all our lives are, one way or another, at root simply *dukkha*. The Buddha was uninterested in the question of God; and Buddhist tradition has been unanimous that a creator-God, in the sense in which he is thought to exist by Christians, for example, simply does not exist. Suffering, for Buddhists, is the result of our ignorance, not understanding the way things really are, and we all live our lives in the light of that failure in understanding. The central dimension of such misunderstanding lies in our not appreciating that everything in our experience is by its very nature impermanent. Alongside impermanence — in fact, logically and doctrinally prior to it — is conditionality: the teaching that things arise and pass away in dependence upon conditions. Suffering results from holding on, trying in our experiences and in our lives to 'fix things' so they do not break up and cease to be. Clearly we are doomed to failure. We need to learn to let go let go of attachment and a fixed sense of selfhood; but this letting go has to occur at a very deep level indeed, since we have been confused and suffering in this manner for infinite lifetimes.

For Buddhists, human experience consists of a flow of consciousness, with associated mental contents such as feelings and intentions, and a body that is ever changing too. Any further unchanging element, called a 'self' (Pali, *atta*; Sanskrit, *atman*), would appear to be unnecessary. Indeed, it could lead to a dangerous form of self-grasping, the very opposite of letting go. Rather, Buddhist tradition teaches 'not-self' (Pali, *anatta*; Sanskrit, *anatman*). At death the body ceases, but the ever-flowing continuum of consciousness and its mental accompaniments continues and 'spins', as it were, another body in accordance with one's good or bad deeds (*karma*). Such 'rebirth' means that one is yet again subject to suffering — old age, sickness, death and so on. This process ceases only with letting go at the deepest possible level, attained through meditation. It is a letting go that springs from seeing things as they truly are, and completely reversing one's almost instinctive and frantic patterns of grasping after things. This cessation Buddhists call 'enlightenment' (Pali, *nibbana*; Sanskrit, *nirvana*).

MONASTIC TRADITIONS AND DOCTRINAL SCHOOLS

Central to the Buddha's vision of the way forward was an order of monks and nuns — known as the *Sangha* — living on alms, and expressing in their state of renunciation their commitment to the radical transformation we all need. In time, monasteries were established, together with a monastic rule, to regulate the conduct of the *Sangha*, and promote the peace and harmony necessary in order to follow the Buddha's path. The Buddha did not appoint a successor, reportedly declaring that the teaching — the *Dharma* — should be his successor. But after his death, with time, disagreements occurred, initially over the monastic rules. Where disputes over the rule could not be reconciled, monks in the minority were required to depart, forming their own groups based on variants of the monastic rule. Eventually, a number of different monastic traditions were formed. The best known of these — and the only one of the early Indian Buddhist monastic traditions to survive to the present day — is the 'Way of the Elders' (*Theravada*), found nowadays in, for example, Sri Lanka, Thailand, Cambodia, and Myanmar (Burma).

In Buddhism, 'schism' (*sanghabheda*) technically concerns monastic rule, not doctrinal disagreement, which is relatively less serious. Nevertheless, as time passed, different doctrinal positions also evolved, sometimes followed by identifiable schools — for example the school known as *Pudgalavada* ('Teaching the *pudgala*'). The point of contention here was that of the 'person' (*pudgala*). Advocates urged that, although the Buddha taught 'not-self', there still exists something – albeit difficult to specify what – called the *pudgala*, as something in some sense really there 'in' us. Others viewed this *pudgala* as just a self in disguise, and an abandonment of a central part of the Buddha's teaching. Further issues of debate involved who or what the Buddha himself was. Some urged that a Buddha is really much more extraordinary than people realize. For example, although he seems to teach, really he is permanently

> *Let none deceive another, not despise any person whatsoever in any place. Let one not wish any harm to another out of anger or ill-will …*
>
> *Let thoughts of boundless love pervade the whole world: above, below and across, without any obstruction, without any hatred, any enmity.*
>
> From the *Metta Sutta, The Discourse on Loving Kindness, Sutta Nipata*, verses 6 and 8

in meditation. He has no need to sleep, to defecate, or even to eat, but only does these things in order to act in accordance with the expectations of the world. Many such topics were debated in early – and even later – Buddhism, as the Buddha's followers sought to put his teaching into practice, and to explain it clearly to others. Indeed, also discussed was the relative importance of practising the *Dharma* for one's own freedom from all suffering, as opposed to compassionately teaching it to others.

WHAT IS MAHAYANA BUDDHISM?

To understand early Buddhist history it is thus necessary to distinguish doctrinal dispute and debate – that is, doctrinal schools – from behavioural disharmony and schism – monastic traditions. Different again, and appearing in the literature from about the first century CE, is the greatest internal development within Buddhism, the growth of the *Mahayana*: the 'Great Vehicle' or perhaps 'the Vehicle that leads to the Great'. Mahayana Buddhism is not a doctrinal school; within the Mahayana there are many doctrinal schools. Moreover the Mahayana is to be distinguished from a monastic tradition. There is no such thing as a distinct set of Mahayana monastic rules (*vinaya*). For example, monks in India holding to the Mahayana perspective would be ordained and live in accordance with any one of the sets of monastic rules that had already developed, and were sometimes to be found in monasteries with others who did not hold to the Mahayana perspective.

Hence it makes no sense to speak of two 'schools' of Buddhism, Theravada and Mahayana. Theravada is a monastic tradition; Mahayana is not. They are not comparable phenomena: there could in theory be a Theravada follower of Mahayana. However, in their practice Mahayana and Theravada are very different phenomena, with different scriptures and practices. Mahayana can best be thought of as a vision of what Buddhism is really, finally, all about. Mahayana appears first in texts – writings known as *Mahayana sutras* – claiming, controversially, to be the word of the Buddha himself. Crucially, what gradually emerges in these writings is a distinction between simply being free from all suffering – in other words, enlightened – and actually being a Buddha. A Buddha is spiritually more than just free from his own suffering; a Buddha is also perfectly compassionate. Thus to be a Buddha is better than simply being enlightened. This is not only because of a Buddha's great compassion,

Stone Buddha in Buddhist temple, Bangkok, Thailand.

but also because of the many marvellous – indeed miraculous – abilities a Buddha possesses in order to help others. But it takes many, many lifetimes of spiritual striving to become a Buddha. Thus, those who aim for the highest goal should seek not just their own freedom from suffering and rebirth, but should also vow to follow the long path to Buddhahood. This path is to be followed over very many rebirths, willingly taking on their attendant sufferings, in order eventually as a Buddha better to be able to help others.

The Mahayana, in a nutshell, is the way of those who aspire to become perfect Buddhas, which is said to be for the benefit of all sentient beings – all those with consciousness. Those who vow to do this are known as *bodhisattvas*, perhaps originally meaning 'one who is capable of awakening'. Mahayana sources go into great detail about the stages of the path that a *bodhisattva* must follow in order to become a Buddha.

With time, the Mahayana also elaborated on the ways in which a Buddha is superior to someone who has simply put an end to his or her own suffering, developing further the idea that a Buddha is really much more than he appears to be. Even his death was just a show, put on in order to give a 'skilful teaching' of impermanence. For the Mahayana, the Buddha – indeed infinite Buddhas – are still around, living on higher planes – 'Pure Lands' – from which, through their great compassion and with miraculous powers, they are available and willing to help those who have need of them. With them are advanced *bodhisattvas*, who are also full of compassion and able to help others. Some of these Buddhas and 'celestial' *bodhisattvas* are named, such as Avalokiteshvara, a *bodhisattva* who is said to be the very incarnation of compassion, or Mañjushri, likewise the very incarnation of wisdom and insight.

BUDDHISM BEYOND INDIA

Significant to the history of Buddhism in India was the conversion of the great Emperor Ashoka (third century BCE), which gave the religion important imperial patronage – although scholars now discount the view that he attempted to make Buddhism the state religion. From the time of Ashoka, Buddhism began to migrate further afield, according

A BRIEF INTRODUCTION TO BUDDHISM

to tradition reaching Sri Lanka at this time. It subsequently spread into South-East Asia, reaching China along the Central Asian trade routes during the early centuries CE, spreading to Korea and other countries of East Asia, and reaching Japan in the sixth century CE. Buddhism came to Tibet from various directions – including India and China – probably from about the seventh century. In India, however, for various reasons not yet fully understood, but possibly partly related to the rise of devotional theistic forms of Hinduism, as well as the impact of Islam on India, Buddhism declined, almost ceasing to exist from about the fourteenth century. It has revived in recent centuries, and Buddhism has also now taken on a global dimension. Perhaps the most well known modern Buddhist is the Dalai Lama of Tibet (1935–), a former winner of the Nobel Peace Prize.

It is common, although misleading, to speak of the Buddhism of, for example, China, Japan, and Tibet as Mahayana, as opposed to the Theravada Buddhism of, for example, South-East Asia. As we have

Buddhist shrine, Macao, Asia.

seen, these are not comparable phenomena. Nevertheless, many Mahayana scriptures were transmitted to, and usually given unquestioning authority in, China, Japan, and Tibet. Unlike in South-East Asia, Buddhists in those countries could be expected to express adherence, in one way or another, to the Mahayana vision as embracing their highest and final aspirations.

ZEN

Particularly characteristic of East Asian Buddhism is the tradition known in Japan as *Zen*. Zen – the word itself is related to 'meditation' – is known for stressing direct, non-verbal, intuitive insight, expressed through arts such as painting, but sometimes also employing humour and shock tactics to bring about awakening. This awakened 'Buddha-nature', it is urged, is already present within all of us, if we did but realize it. Also important in, for example, Japanese Buddhism is the tradition of Shinran (thirteenth century CE). For Shinran, the awakening of a Buddha is quite beyond unenlightened capabilities; only by completely letting go of reliance on ourselves, and trusting in the Buddha's salvific ability, can the already-enlightened nature of the Buddha (a Buddha known here as *Amida*) shine

BUDDHISM TIMELINE

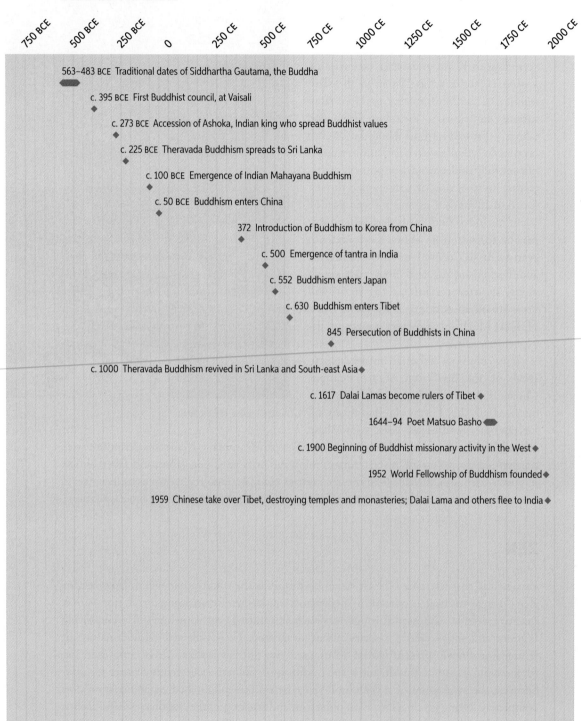

750 BCE   500 BCE   250 BCE   0   250 CE   500 CE   750 CE   1000 CE   1250 CE   1500 CE   1750 CE   2000 CE

563–483 BCE Traditional dates of Siddhartha Gautama, the Buddha

c. 395 BCE First Buddhist council, at Vaisali

c. 273 BCE Accession of Ashoka, Indian king who spread Buddhist values

c. 225 BCE Theravada Buddhism spreads to Sri Lanka

c. 100 BCE Emergence of Indian Mahayana Buddhism

c. 50 BCE Buddhism enters China

372 Introduction of Buddhism to Korea from China

c. 500 Emergence of tantra in India

c. 552 Buddhism enters Japan

c. 630 Buddhism enters Tibet

845 Persecution of Buddhists in China

c. 1000 Theravada Buddhism revived in Sri Lanka and South-east Asia

c. 1617 Dalai Lamas become rulers of Tibet

1644–94 Poet Matsuo Basho

c. 1900 Beginning of Buddhist missionary activity in the West

1952 World Fellowship of Buddhism founded

1959 Chinese take over Tibet, destroying temples and monasteries; Dalai Lama and others flee to India

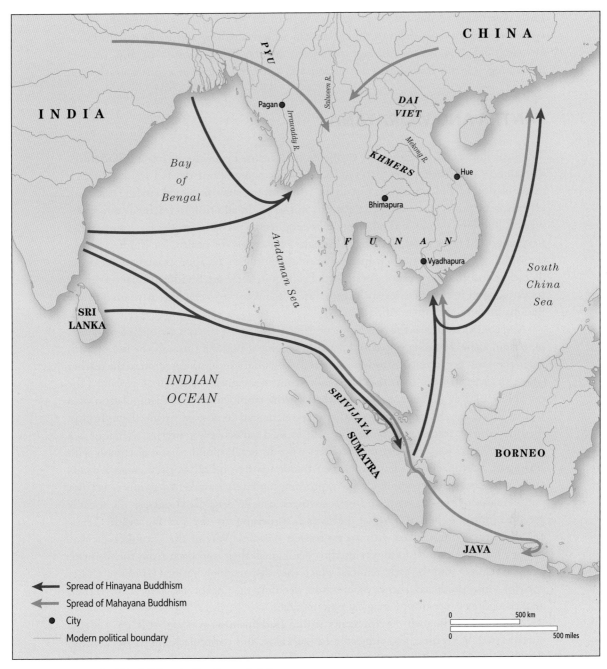

Spread of Buddhism to South-east Asia

Legend:
- Spread of Hinayana Buddhism
- Spread of Mahayana Buddhism
- City
- Modern political boundary

CHINA

INDIA

PYU

Bay of Bengal

Irrawaddy R.

Salween R.

Pagan

DAI VIET

Mekong R.

KHMERS

Hue

Bhimapura

F U N A N

Vyadhapura

Andaman Sea

South China Sea

SRI LANKA

INDIAN OCEAN

SRIVIJAYA

SUMATRA

BORNEO

JAVA

0   500 km
0   500 miles

forth. According to this teaching, humans have to let go completely of even the subtle egoism that encourages them to think they can achieve anything spiritually worthwhile – including enlightenment – through their own efforts. Being a monk or nun, or even meditating, is finally irrelevant, a distraction, and a possible source of egoistic attachment.

TANTRA AND VAJRAYANA

The final important development to mention is *Tantra*. From the beginning Buddhists, in common with their peers, accepted magic – bringing about desired results through manipulation of hidden forces, usually by ritual means such as sacred circles (*mandalas*), utterances of power (*mantras*), visualizations and so on. In addition to teaching, among the services Buddhist monks and nuns might be required to perform for the lay communities that supported them would be magical rituals – for crops, for health, for children and so on. Although this was not their main interest as Buddhists, its appropriateness, as an act of caring, and efficacy was not questioned. From quite early on, Buddhist ritual texts were produced, and in some circles such texts were – again controversially – attributed to the Buddha himself, and often called *tantras*.

Also controversial was the development, from perhaps the seventh century CE or earlier, of certain *tantras* claiming one could actually become a Buddha through the use of such magical means. Secret initiations were required, with unquestioning devotion to the teacher (*guru*), in order to learn their use. Even more controversial were *tantras* that explained the possibility of this supreme attainment through the employment and manipulation of a sort of subtle, psycho-physical body that everyone is said to possess within them. In this, the ritual use of sexual intercourse was held to be a particularly powerful technique – a practice reserved for advanced practitioners who do not respond to sexual stimuli with craving or attachment. Since an awakened Buddha is beyond all worldly entanglements and confusions, also recommended – expressing humanity's awakened nature – are not only sexual activity – in ways, and with partners, usually considered outside the socially accepted norm – but also other behaviour surprising to the unenlightened. These developments – often linked with the expression *Vajrayana* (Way of the Thunderbolt, Way of the Diamond), which followers used to distinguish their approach from the *Mahayana* (the Great Way), and the early schools, which they disparagingly termed '*Hinayana*' (lesser vehicle) – also produced a genre of literature detailing the unexpected exploits of certain awakened tantric 'persons of magical power' (*siddhas*).

Not surprisingly, such developments within Buddhism were – and still are – highly controversial. With time, and subjected to orthodox, and particularly monastic, control, the more controversial dimensions of Tantric Buddhism were 'tamed' and absorbed into the wider Mahayana spiritual context of great compassion and wisdom. It is in this form that one finds today the widest and most well known presence of *tantra*, in the Buddhism of Tibet.

PAUL WILLIAMS

CHAPTER 10

Sacred Writings

The Buddha himself wrote nothing; he simply taught. He sometimes taught his vision of the world, humanity's place within it, and the spiritual and moral way to freedom — eventually complete freedom — from incompleteness, frustration, and suffering. At other times he settled disputes among his followers, or legislated for the best sort of life to live to attain this complete freedom. According to Buddhist tradition, soon after the Buddha's death those monks who had achieved the goal — enlightenment (Pali, *nibbana*; Sanskrit, *nirvana*) — met to recite what they remembered of the Buddha's discourses at the First Buddhist Council. (It is often stated there were three such councils in classical times, although only two are accepted by all Buddhist traditions.)

ORAL TRANSMISSION

The emphasis from the beginning was on memory and recitation. For the first few centuries, the Buddhist scriptures were handed down orally — which partly explains the importance in Buddhism of the oral transmission from teacher to pupil — rather than in written form. Different groups of monks specialized in preserving different texts, or collections of scriptures; and transmission through oral recitation in groups proved to be a very effective way of preserving the Buddha's words — at least as accurate as writing, since interpolation of additional — and perhaps controversial — material or omission is much more difficult, as it would immediately be noticed. According to one Buddhist tradition, the scriptures were not written down until the first century BCE. The decision to resort to writing was perhaps partly due to fear in time of social and political stress that the teachings might become lost through the death of significant numbers of important reciters by disease, war, or famine — something that seems to have happened, for example, with some of the scriptures of Jainism.

THE BUDDHIST CANON

The texts recited at the First Council form the basis of the Buddhist scriptural canon. They are divided into:

sutras (Pali, *sutta*) – the general discourses of the Buddha and, sometimes, the teachings of his authorized followers

vinaya – texts relating to the structure and discipline of the monastic order.

With time, a further section of the canon was added, the *abhidharma* (Pali, *abhidhamma*): perhaps 'higher [or 'more precise'] teaching'. This section consists mainly of works that develop an elaborate description of how the psycho-physical world looks when seen 'as things really are' by an enlightened person, rather than through everyday unenlightened vision. The canonical *abhidharma* texts probably date from after the death of the Buddha, but all claim direct origin from him.

These three sections together form the 'Three Baskets' (Pali, *Tipitaka*; Sanskrit, *Tripitaka*), which are themselves subdivided. For example, in the Pali Canon, the *sutra* 'basket' is divided into four sections – plus one supplementary section – known as *Nikayas*. Perhaps the best known of these is the 'Collection of Long Discourses' (*Digha Nikaya*).

It was some centuries before the canon became more or less closed, such that – at least in theory – no more works could be added to it and given the prestige of 'coming directly from the Buddha himself'. Some scholars think the *Sutta Pitaka* was closed 150 years after the Buddha, while the other sections were closed later. There are also some Buddhist texts which have all the authority of canonical scriptures, but are not technically part of the canon at all – for example the monastic rule, still recited regularly by monks and nuns.

DIFFERENT VERSIONS

There is a tradition that the Buddha recommended preserving and transmitting his teachings in local languages rather than Sanskrit, the pan-Indian language of education. Hence, from quite early times, Buddhist scriptures were in a number of languages and also underwent translation. Moreover, as the various Buddhist monastic traditions and doctrinal schools were formed, different versions of the canon began to appear, often in different Indian languages. Nowadays, the comparative study of different canonical versions of recognizably the same text forms a fruitful area of scholarly research.

Scriptures require some sort of authoritative body to preserve and transmit them down the ages. In Buddhism, particularly in the Indian world, this has always been the monastic order, the *Sangha*. The only Buddhist monastic tradition to have survived from the early centuries to the present day is the 'Way of the Elders' (*Theravada*); the canon preserved by the *Theravada* – the sole version to have survived in its entirety and in its ancient Indian language – is the 'Pali Canon', written in the *Pali* language. Although old – and of inestimable importance for the study of Buddhism – the Pali Canon is only one of a number of Buddhist canons that existed in ancient times. Other individual canonical works, or collections, have survived, either in other Indian languages, or in ancient translations, for example into Chinese or Tibetan, made as part of Buddhist missionary activity.

With time, and with greater reliance on writing than on oral transmission, certain Buddhist traditions and schools in India started to preserve their scriptures in Sanskrit, which is why Buddhist terms are often given in both their Sanskrit and Pali forms — usually very similar: for example, *nibbana* (Pali), *nirvana* (Sanskrit). As Buddhism spread across India, using just one language made sense, rather than relying on different translations in different areas. Educated people would be familiar with Sanskrit, and a monk with a Sanskrit text could take it anywhere, without needing to have it translated, explaining in the vernacular what the text meant to less educated people as part of his teaching mission. This change to the use of Sanskrit can be seen occurring in the greatest post-canonical scriptural development in Indian Buddhism, the appearance of the Mahayana *sutras*. A number of the early Mahayana *sutras* show signs of having been translated into Sanskrit out of other Indian languages, in which, presumably, they were originally composed.

Stupa (dome) of the ninth-century CE Mahayana Buddhist temple of Borobudur, or Barabudur, Magelang, Central Java, Indonesia.

APOCRYPHAL SCRIPTURES

The earliest form in which we know Mahayana Buddhism is in its scriptures. Indeed, for followers of Mahayana, scriptural support appears to be older by some centuries than archaeological evidence. Mahayana *sutras* are apocryphal, and their ideas often seemingly new and radical. As apocryphal *sutras*, although they claim to be the words of the Buddha himself, this claim is hotly disputed within Buddhism, and the extant versions of these *sutras* cannot possibly be that old. Elements of at least some early Mahayana *sutras* may have originated in inspiring, meditative visions and revelations, held to be from a Buddha, who was thus thought to be still accessible to us on some 'higher plane'.

Although there may have been attempts to add such *sutras*, they are not included in any official canon preserved by any known Indian monastic tradition.

Apocryphal *sutras* were not created in India alone. For example, many Mahayana apocryphal *sutras* were composed in China, and unknown in India in classical times. Even today, outside areas usually associated with Mahayana – for example, the monastically Theravada world of Sri Lanka – apocryphal Buddhist *sutras* are still produced, claiming to spring from some sort of special revelation, but not accepted as canonical by the mainstream, local Buddhist monastic order.

It has been suggested that the origin and survival of Mahayana as a movement required the existence of writing. Religions often produce controversial texts claiming to be the words of, or in some sense inspired by, their founder; but such works disappear unless taken up and preserved by enthusiasts down the ages. In traditional Buddhism, canonical works have been preserved and transmitted to future generations by the monastic *Sangha*. But the *Sangha* was unlikely to preserve apocryphal texts, and certainly not texts such as the early Mahayana *sutras*, which inclined sometimes to be critical of the existing monastic hierarchy. Hence, so long as the canon was transmitted orally, the preservation of significant new perspectives – such as that of Mahayana, claiming the authority of the Buddha – was all but impossible. However, the writing down of the scriptures made possible the preservation and transmission of apocryphal works and perspectives. A written text could survive, providing someone was willing to preserve it.

TANTRAS

The other major corpus of apocryphal, scriptural literature in Buddhism claiming the authority of the Buddha himself consists of the *Tantras*, texts associated with the use of ritual magic. Their origins in Buddhism – they are also found in Hinduism and Jainism – are obscure, and the earliest *Tantras* are certainly some centuries later than the earliest Mahayana *sutras*. This literature is very large. To practise the ritual prescriptions of these texts, which in time came to include techniques for attaining enlightenment as well as more mundane magical activities, requires initiation, close instruction from a teacher (*guru*), and vows of secrecy. Tantric texts involve the use of such methods as magical diagrams, utterances (*mantras*), and visualizations. *Tantras* have become linked with, and in places such as Tibet assimilated into, Mahayana; but recent research has also found tantric literature in Myanmar (Burma) and Cambodia, countries not normally associated with Mahayana perspectives.

> *Asked by some citizens of Kalama for guidance, the Buddha said: 'Be not led by reports or tradition or hearsay. Be not led by the authority of religious texts, nor by mere logic or inference, nor by considering appearances … But, O Kalamas, when you know for yourselves that certain things are unwholesome* (akusala) *and wrong and bad, then give them up … And when you know for yourselves that certain things are wholesome* (kusala) *and good, then accept them and follow them.'*
>
> *Anguttara Nikaya 3.65 (i 188).*

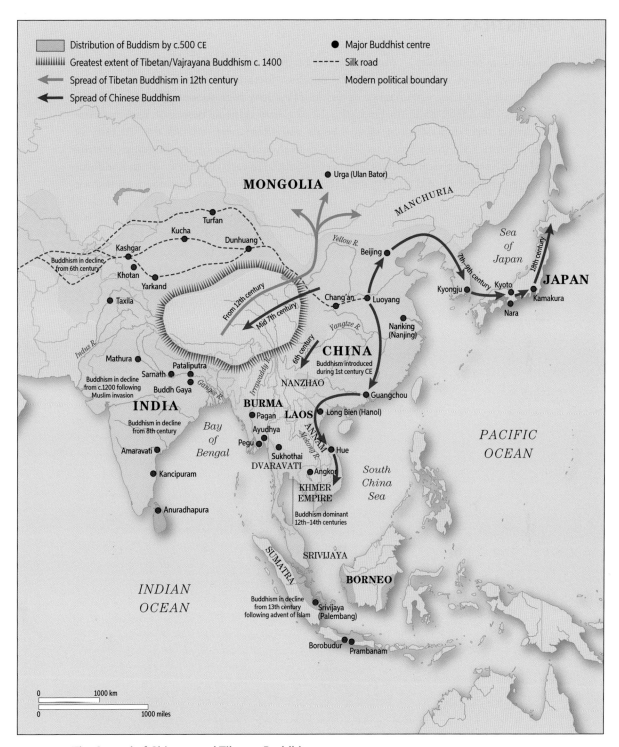

Legend:

Distribution of Buddism by c.500 CE

Greatest extent of Tibetan/Vajrayana Buddhism c. 1400

Spread of Tibetan Buddhism in 12th century

Spread of Chinese Buddhism

● Major Buddhist centre

- - - Silk road

Modern political boundary

MONGOLIA

Urga (Ulan Bator)

MANCHURIA

Turfan

Kucha

Dunhuang

Kashgar

Yellow R.

Beijing

Sea of Japan

Khotan

Yarkand

Buddhism in decline from 6th century

Chang'an

Luoyang

Kyongju

7th–9th century

Kyoto

18th century

JAPAN

Kamakura

Nara

Taxila

From 12th century

Mid 7th century

Yangtze R.

Nanking (Nanjing)

Indus R.

Mathura

Pataliputra

Sarnath

6th century

CHINA

Buddhism introduced during 1st century CE

Buddh Gaya

Buddhism in decline from c.1200 following Muslim invasion

Ganges R.

NANZHAO

Guangchou

INDIA

Buddhism in decline from 8th century

Amaravati

Kancipuram

Anuradhapura

BURMA

Pagan

Ayudhya

Pegu

Sukhothai

DVARAVATI

Angkor

Irrawaddy R.

Bay of Bengal

LAOS

Long Bien (Hanoi)

ANNAM

Hue

Mekong R.

KHMER EMPIRE

Buddhism dominant 12th–14th centuries

South China Sea

PACIFIC OCEAN

INDIAN OCEAN

SUMATRA

SRIVIJAYA

BORNEO

Buddhism in decline from 13th century following advent of Islam

Srivijaya (Palembang)

Borobudur

Prambanam

0   1000 km

0   1000 miles

The Spread of Chinese and Tibetan Buddhism

SHASTRAS

In addition to scriptures – those accepted by all as canonical, and those of disputed authority, held by some as apocryphal – Buddhist literature also includes a vast number of exegetical treatises, often known as *shastras*. These have been produced by great scholars of various Buddhist traditions and schools, to clarify difficult points of interpretation, to defend their understanding against rivals and alternatives, or, like the 'Treasury of Abhidharma' (*Abhidharmakosha*), to serve as critical compendia of the Buddhist doctrine and path. Such exegetical treatises have been produced in each country in which Buddhism has been established, and are very important for the study of Buddhist doctrinal history.

PAUL WILLIAMS

CHAPTER II

Beliefs

A disciple of the Buddha, Malunkyaputta, complained that the Buddha had not answered some of the most important questions of life – Is the world eternal? Is the soul the same as the body? and so on. The Buddha replied with a story.

> *A man is wounded by an arrow thickly smeared with poison. His friends and relatives brought a surgeon to him. The man said, 'I will not let the surgeon pull out this arrow until I know whether the man who wounded me was a noble, a brahman, a merchant or a worker. I will not let the surgeon pull out the arrow until I know the name and clan of the man who wounded me ... until I know whether the he was tall or short or of middle height ... until I know whether the bow that wounded me was a longbow or a crossbow ... until I know whether the bowstring that wounded me was fibre or reed or sinew or bark ...*
>
> *All this would not be known to the man and he would die.*
>
> Abridged from the *Culamalunkya Sutta, Majjhima Nikaya 63* (I, 246).

So, the Buddha added, will those die who insist they must know the answers to speculative questions about the nature of reality before starting to live the holy life. For such questions are not beneficial to the real task, the cessation of suffering.

This story points to the heart of what Buddhism is about. Buddhism is less a set of beliefs than a path, leading from suffering to the cessation of suffering, from ignorance to compassion and wisdom. The Buddha's first invitation to those who wished to follow him as monks or nuns in the fifth century BCE was: 'Come, live the holy life, in order that you make an end of suffering.' The only credal statement in Buddhism, therefore, is:

> *I go to the Buddha for refuge;*
> *I go to the Dhamma for refuge;*
> *I go to the* Sangha *[the Buddhist community] for refuge.*

These are the 'Three Jewels' or 'Three Gems': anyone who places them at the centre of life, by 'going for refuge' to them, is a Buddhist. The *Dhamma* (Pali; Sanskrit, *Dharma*) – literally, 'that which constitutes', or 'the way things are' – is what the Buddha 'awoke to' at his enlightenment, and what he taught for forty years after. For Buddhists, it is the truth about the nature of existence; the truth that upholds the cosmos; the truth that all Buddhas have taught. Across the different schools of Buddhism, the *Dhamma* is expressed in a variety of ways; however, there are elements that all schools hold in common.

LIVING THE HOLY LIFE

Living the holy life involves a way of seeing reality and a way of acting. The way of seeing begins with experience rather than metaphysics: the experience that something in life is dislocated, flawed, unsatisfactory, and full of suffering, and the realization that one reason for this is that everything is impermanent. We are separated from loved ones. We lose our strength. We grow old, sicken, and die. Everything we cherish – youth, strength, possessions, relationships – passes away. Buddhism speaks of three defining characteristics of existence: impermanence (Pali, *anicca*; Sanskrit, *anitya*), unsatisfactoriness (Pali, *dukkha*; Sanskrit, *duhkha*), and not-self (Pali, *anatta*; Sanskrit, *anatman*). The characteristic of not-self arises when the concept of impermanence is applied to the self. As with all external phenomena, everything in our bodies and minds is changing, everything is conditioned. There is no unchanging 'self', 'soul', or ego. Mahayana Buddhists use the word 'emptiness'. All things – the self included – are 'empty' of their own nature.

> *Whatever harm an enemy may do to an enemy, or a hater to a hater, an ill-directed mind inflicts on oneself a greater harm.*
>
> Dhammapada, v. 42

This is the start of the Buddhist view of existence, but not the end. The message of the Buddha was that the suffering or unsatisfactoriness of life is not haphazard, random, or immovable. It has a cause, as all other phenomena have a cause, and if this cause is eradicated, suffering will not arise. The cause abides within the mind, and the Buddha identified it as 'craving': self-centred desire for sensual pleasures and life itself. Remove this craving, and suffering will cease, giving way to the liberation of *nibbana* (Sanskrit, *nirvana*). It is this 'view' that forms the first three of the Four Noble Truths:

- The Noble Truth of *Dukkha*: that there is an incompleteness and unsatisfactoriness at the heart of existence;
- The Noble Truth of the Origin of *Dukkha*: that the cause is craving or thirst (Pali, *tanha*; Sanskrit, *trsna*), the thirst for sensual pleasures, the thirst for continued existence, and the thirst for annihilation;
- The Noble Truth of the Cessation of *Dukkha*: that there is an end, based on the law of cause and effect – that is, if craving is destroyed, *dukkha* cannot arise;
- The Noble Truth of the Path to the Cessation of *Dukkha*: the Eightfold Path (see below).

The Buddhist view of the world is, therefore, of a world dis-eased (that is, ill at ease), a world entrapped in craving, where *dukkha* reigns supreme because people have not seen the *dhamma*, the truth about existence. It is a world where people are trapped in mental prisons of their own making. But it is a world where liberation awaits all who can change the way they look at the world and work towards freedom from the craving that is rooted in ignorance and expressed through greed and hatred.

THE WAY TO LIBERATION

The Noble Truths are the 'house' into which everything else fits in Buddhism.

The Fourth Noble Truth is the Noble Eightfold Path, the way to the ending of suffering:
- right view
- right resolve
- right speech
- right action
- right livelihood
- right effort
- right mindfulness
- right concentration or meditation

This is often reduced to just three categories: morality (Pali/Sanskrit, *sila*); concentration or meditation (Pali/Sanskrit, *samadhi*); and wisdom (Pali, *panna*; Sanskrit, *prajna*). Sometimes the following verse from the *Dhammapada*, a text known and loved throughout the Buddhist world, is quoted:

> *The avoidance of evil, the undertaking of good, the cleansing of one's mind;*
> *this is the teaching of the awakened ones.*

Dhammapada, v. 183

MORALITY

Morality is the bedrock of the Buddhist path. It involves 'the avoidance of evil, the undertaking of good'. Without moral discipline, the holy life cannot be lived. Most lay Buddhists place the following five precepts at the centre of their life:
- to abstain from harming any living being
- to abstain from taking what is not given
- to abstain from sexual misconduct
- to abstain from false speech
- to abstain from anything that clouds or intoxicates the mind, such as drugs and alcohol.

Many would insist that these precepts involve not only abstention, but cultivation. A commitment not to harm involves the development of loving-kindness and compassion. The commitment to abstaining from taking what is not given involves recognizing the dignity and worth of other people, as does abstaining from sexual misconduct. Abstaining from false speech involves cultivating honesty and integrity.

An ancient text in the Theravada tradition, the *Karaniyametta Sutta*, describes loving-kindness in the following way: 'Just as a mother would protect her only child at the risk of her own life, even so cultivate a boundless heart towards all beings.' One way to do this is to meditate on loving-kindness (*metta*). The first step is to imagine oneself surrounded by loving-kindness. Then this loving-kindness — sometimes imagined as a white, warm light — is thrown further and further outwards into the world. First of all those dear to the meditator are brought to mind. Then the radius widens, eventually reaching those who are disliked, or even hated. It is a transformative practice that spills into everyday conduct.

Morality, for many Buddhists, is also linked with the law of action, the law of *karma* (Sanskrit; Pali, *kamma*), that moral action will produce good fruit, and unwholesome action bad fruit. This does not mean Buddhist morality is essentially selfish. Rather, self and other are seen to be interconnected. What is good for others is good for self; what would not be done to oneself would not be done to another.

The Golden Buddha, Phra Phuttha Maha Suwan Patimakon, is the world's largest solid gold statue, and sited at the Temple of Wat Traimit, Bangkok, Thailand. It was created roughly 700 years ago.

MEDITATION

The task of meditation is to cleanse the mind. It ties in with the heart of the Buddha's message: that the cause of our dis-ease lies in our craving, in the three unwholesome roots of greed, hatred, and delusion. Since it is our minds and hearts that generate this craving, according to Buddhism, the only way to uproot craving is to work on the mind and heart. Buddhism offers numerous meditation methods, but these can be reduced to two main practices: tranquillity meditation (Pali/Sanskrit, *samatha*) and insight meditation (Pali, *vipassana*; Sanskrit, *vipasyana*).

Tranquillity meditation is not unique to Buddhism. It is a method through which an object of meditation is used to concentrate the mind and gain one-pointedness. The most popular object is the breath: some Buddhists pay attention to the breath as it enters and leaves the nostrils; others watch the rise and fall of the abdomen. The meditator sits with the back upright; in some traditions the eyes are closed, in others they remain partly open. When the mind wanders away from the object, it is brought back, gently and non-judgmentally, to the breath. Traditionally, forty other meditation objects can be chosen, under the direction of a teacher. This kind of meditation may lead to what Buddhists call 'meditative absorptions' or *jhanas* (Pali; Sanskrit, *dhyanas*), states of intense absorption and mental refinement.

Vipassana means 'seeing clearly' – seeing the body and the mind clearly – and is unique to Buddhism, and distinct from altered states of consciousness. Its aim is direct verification of the *Dhamma* through observation of the body and the mind. Many exercises have been developed within the Buddhist tradition to aid this. One method used widely is 'bare attention', or 'choiceless awareness', a form of mindfulness that emphasizes the present moment. Whatever arises in the mind and the body becomes the object of meditation, of awareness. It may be a reaction of attraction or aversion to an external noise, a feeling of pain in the legs, or thoughts of hatred, jealousy, or love. Nothing is judged good or bad, nothing clung to. Everything is watched, noted, and allowed to pass; its impermanence and not-self seen. The

The Pure Mind

All that we are is the result of what we have thought: it is founded on our thoughts, it is made up of our thoughts. If a man speaks or acts with an evil thought, pain follows him, as the wheel follows the foot of the ox that draws the carriage.

All that we are is the result of what we have thought: it is founded on our thoughts, it is made up of our thoughts. If a man speaks or acts with a pure thought, happiness follows him, like a shadow that never leaves him.

'He abused me, he beat me, he defeated me, he robbed me' – in those who harbour such thoughts hatred will never cease.

'He abused me, he beat me, he defeated me, he robbed me,' – in those who do not harbour such thoughts hatred will cease.

For hatred does not cease by hatred at any time: hatred ceases by love, this is an old rule.

The world does not know that we must all come to an end here: but those who know it, their quarrels cease at once.

He who lives looking for pleasures only, his senses uncontrolled, immoderate in his food, idle, and weak, Mara (death) will certainly overthrow him, as the wind throws down a weak tree.

He who lives without looking for pleasures, his senses well controlled, moderate in his food, faithful and strong, him Mara will certainly not overthrow, any more than the wind throws down a rocky mountain.

The Dhammapada 1.1–8, transl. by Max Müller and Max Fausböll, 1881, adapted.

greed, hatred, and delusion in everything is seen, as well as what triggers them. Each period of meditation becomes a voyage of discovery into the way the mind and body function. Other methods include noticing the impermanent or insubstantial nature of experience, and dismantling the experience of selfhood by examining it in the light of Buddhist teachings.

Thai Buddhist temple.

Buddhists believe meditation is the principal means through which greed, hatred, and delusion or ignorance can be uprooted and transcended. Central to 'delusion' (Pali, *moha*) is the belief that we have an unchanging 'I' or ego that has to be placed at the centre of all things, to be protected, promoted, and pampered. Meditation shows that the things we believe to be 'self' — our feelings, our thoughts, our pain — are impermanent and empty.

REBIRTH

Buddhists stress that there is continuity after death, but that the ultimate goal of religious practice is not an after-death state. The term most often used is 'rebirth', which most Buddhists prefer to 'reincarnation', since they do not believe there is an unchanging soul

A BRIEF INTRODUCTION TO BUDDHISM

to reincarnate, but rather an ever-changing process of cause and effect. Death is believed to lead continually to rebirth after rebirth, until greed, hatred, and delusion are eradicated. For the Theravada Buddhist, one can be reborn into any of five realms:

1. the hells;
2. the animal world;
3. the realm of the hungry ghosts;
4. the realm of humans; and
5. the realm of the gods.

Mahayana Buddhists have added another heavenly realm:

6. that of the demi-gods.

> Monks, there are to be seen beings who can admit freedom from suffering from bodily disease for one year, for two years, for three, four, five, ten, twenty, thirty, forty, fifty years; who can admit freedom from bodily disease for even a hundred years. But, monks, those beings are hard to find in the world who can admit freedom from mental disease even for one moment, save only those in whom the asavas ('corruptions' such as ignorance) are destroyed.
>
> *Anguttara Nikaya* Text ii, 143.

Each realm is linked to a particular emotion or characteristic, and they are states of mind as well as states of being. So one who is in the grip of hatred and anger is, in one sense, already in the hell realm.

The goal of the Buddhist path is to go beyond all of these realms by attaining *nirvana*, through eradicating greed, hatred, and delusion. Some Buddhists see this as a well-nigh impossible immediate goal. For them, rebirth in a heavenly realm, through following the five precepts and developing loving kindness, is goal enough. Others insist that *nirvana* is possible in this very life. Whether it is seen as possible now, or in the distant future, all Buddhists speak of it with joy and wonder. *Nirvana* is the end of suffering and rebirth, attained when the fire of craving is put out. It is the highest ethical state, but also beyond all human ethical constructs. It is defined by wisdom and compassion, yet beyond anything that the unenlightened person can conceive. It is absolute security and bliss. It is liberation. Some Mahayana Buddhists link it with realizing one's Buddha nature. Theravada Buddhists speak of reaching the state of the *arahat*. What happens after death to those who have realized their Buddha nature, or reached the state of the *arahat*, is left open. The message of the texts is that it is beyond all human concepts.

Some Buddhists in the Mahayana tradition have an additional goal: the liberation of all beings. They take what is known as the *bodhisattva* vow, an aspiration to achieve enlightenment not for oneself alone, but for the sake of all beings. This is sometimes envisaged as a commitment to stay within the realm of birth and rebirth until all beings have been liberated.

ELIZABETH J. HARRIS

CHAPTER 12

Family and Society

The original call of the Buddha was: 'Come, live the holy life in order that you make an end of suffering.' Some who heard this renounced home and family to become celibate monks and nuns (Pali, *bhikkhus, bhikkhunis*; Sanskrit, *bhiksu, bhiksuni*). Others remained within their family as lay followers. A clear division emerged between the two, summed up in the verse from the Pali Canon about the peacock and the swan:

The blue-necked peacock which flies through the air never approaches the speed of the swan. Similarly, the householder can never resemble the monk who is endowed with the qualities of a sage who meditates, aloof, in the jungle.

Sutta Nipata, v. 221

THE FOURFOLD SOCIETY

Those with no responsibilities to their families were believed to be on the fast track to *nirvana*, because they could more easily free themselves from attachments, and from the attraction and aversion that attachments generate. Householders, generally speaking, were on the slower track, forced into wealth creation and worries about survival. However, that did not mean they were unimportant, or that they could not reach high levels of religious purity. The canonical texts contain many examples of strong, spiritual laypeople. Early Buddhism spoke about the 'Fourfold Society – monks, nuns, laymen, and laywomen – with a relationship of interdependence between them:

- Monks and nuns were dependent for food and other requisites on laypeople.
- Householders were taught the *dhamma* (Pali; Sanskrit, *dharma*) by the ordained, and gained a 'field' for the making of merit (Pali: *punna*; Sanskrit, *punya*). The concept of merit derives from the law of action (Pali, *kamma*; Sanskrit, *karma*), according to which good action produces good

> *Just as a mother would protect her only child at the risk of her own life, even so cultivate a boundless heart towards all beings.*
>
> From *The Discourse on Loving Kindness, Sutta Nipata, v. 149*

consequences. Monks and nuns were a 'field' for merit-gaining, because good consequences were ensured for any who were generous to them.

This fourfold system still exists in many Asian countries with a Buddhist majority. The order of nuns was lost in countries such as Sri Lanka and Myanmar (Burma), but action by Buddhist women in recent decades is bringing it back. In the twentieth century, Buddhist movements without orders of traditional monks or nuns developed, such as Rissho Kosei-kai and Soka Gakkai in Japan, and the Friends of the Western Triratna Buddhist Order in Britain and elsewhere. However, the last distinguishes between 'members' – *Dharmacari* and *Dharmacarini* – male and female 'followers of the *Dharma*' – who follow a limited rule of discipline – and 'friends'. However, the majority of Buddhists still operate within a system in which there is a clear distinction between those who renounce family ties and the laity.

Yet, when Buddhist societies are compared to each other, there is tremendous variety. As Buddhism spread from India, it became rooted in diverse cultures. Buddhism in Japan and China, for example, feels very different, culturally,

Young Buddhist mendicant monks in Luang Prabang, Laos.

from Buddhism in Sri Lanka. Globalizing forces, and the entry of Buddhism into the West, are causing more changes, as Buddhists adapt, innovate, and sometimes retrench. To generalize about family and society within Buddhism is therefore difficult.

FAMILY

In all Buddhist communities, the family is most important. However, in most traditional Buddhist societies, marriage is a secular matter. It is linked with the worldly, and takes place without the presence of a religious officiant. There is no concept of sacred vows made before God, since Buddhism is not a theistic religion in the strict sense of the word. For the same reason, divorce in some Buddhist communities — at least before the period of European colonialism — was a straightforward, mundane matter, that gave rights to the wife unknown to Western women at the time. Under the influence of colonialism, Christianity, and globalization, changes have occurred. Some Buddhist brides in Sri Lanka, for instance, now wear white, a colour traditionally linked with funerals and sterility. Religious verses are sung during the ceremony, and occasionally monks are involved. Also, divorce has become much more difficult.

Children are greeted with joy. Although there is a recognition that the love and attachment connected with parenting has a cost, and is a cause of pain (*dukkha*), positive images of parenthood permeate all schools of Buddhism. Because of the Buddhist belief in rebirth, children are seen as coming into the world with a history. They are not the parents' 'possession', for they have had previous lives. There is also a belief that human life is precious, a not-to-be-missed opportunity to progress spiritually. In the Tibetan tradition especially, focusing on the preciousness of human life is part of meditation practice.

Family relationships, according to one ancient Theravada text, the *Sigalovada Sutta*, are to be regulated according to reciprocal sets of duties that almost touch on the modern concept of human rights. Wives are to offer hospitality to the extended family, show faithfulness, look after the goods brought by their husbands, and carry out their duties with skill. Husbands should in turn show respect, courtesy, and faithfulness, give authority to their wives, and provide 'adornments' such as clothing and jewellery. Servants are to do their work well and rise before their employers, but employers in turn are to assign their employees work according to their strength, look after them in sickness, supply them with food and wages, and give them leave. Times have changed since this discourse was written, but its underlying ideals remain influential in Buddhist families and in the wider society, particularly in Theravada countries.

> To those in the kingdom who are engaged in cultivating crops and raising cattle, let your majesty distribute grain and fodder; to those in trade, give capital; to those in government service assign proper living wages.
>
> Advice given to a king troubled by lawlessness, from the *Kutadanta Sutta*, *Digha Nikaya*, 5: I 135.

SOCIETY

The traditional Buddhist image of the state is of a monarch, influenced by the *Dhamma* and advised by the monastic *Sangha* (community), creating wellbeing in society through a wise legal system and economic justice — ensuring the poor have a means of livelihood, for instance. The spread of democratic models has changed this, although in some countries the monastic *Sangha* still sees itself as an adviser to the state. It could be argued, however, that Buddhism has always had a democratic model to offer — the monastic *Sangha*, inspiration for which could have come from some of the more republican models of governance in the Buddha's own society. Today Buddhism is practised within a number of different political models.

One stereotype of Buddhism is that it encourages withdrawal from society, because of its emphasis on non-attachment. This is misleading: for the Buddhist, non-attachment is non-attachment to all that plays havoc in society: selfishness, greed, hatred, anger, violence, and jealousy. It has nothing to do with lack of compassion or apathy. In fact, one of the contributions Buddhism offer to the world is its emphasis on the compassion and lovingkindness that can flow when greed and hatred, jealousy and competitiveness, are controlled and transcended. One of the first steps is the ability to empathize with others:

> *All tremble at violence; to all life is dear. Comparing [others] with oneself, one should not kill nor cause others to kill.*

> Dhammapada, v. 130

ELIZABETH J. HARRIS

THE CAO DAI AND THE HOA HAO

In the late nineteenth and early twentieth centuries, Vietnamese nationalism was firmly, sometimes harshly, repressed by colonial French occupiers. The intellectuals who traditionally led nationalist movements began in the 1920s to profit financially from the situation and to enjoy privileged status like the French. Organizations then arose under new forms of nationalist leadership, seeking to end French domination and to establish a republic. Some of them followed Communist principles, but three were under the religious leadership of monks and priests: the Cao Dai, the Hoa Hao and, less important, the Binh Xuyen. All three feared and hated things foreign. They were products of local education, and aimed not only at expelling foreigners but also establishing local rule by religious leaders – something quite new to the Vietnamese pattern of rule by the privileged.

During the 1930s, the Communist Party of Indo-China (CPI) began to gain sympathy abroad. At this point the three religious movements began armed opposition to the French colonial forces. The Cao Dai held the Mekong Delta, the Hoa Hao the border of Cambodia, and the Binh Xuyen the Saigon area.

From 1941 until the end of World War II, Japanese military commanders directed the French colonial forces for the Vichy government in France. For a brief period in 1941, the combined French and Japanese all but defeated the local troops; but during the remainder of the war the latter gained strength. After the final defeat of the Japanese, the USA – in the grip of anti-colonial convictions – aided the Communist-controlled Viet Minh, led by Ho Chi Minh (1890–1969), and Vietnamese independence was declared on 2 September 1945.

Because American and French interests in Vietnam were at variance, a decade of confused political, cultural, and religious action and reaction resulted, leading finally to the Geneva Accord of 1954 and the partition of North and South Vietnam. The Communist Viet Minh held the North, while the South was under the nationalist government of Ngo Dinh Diem (1901–63). Close on a million refugees from North to South added to the confusion. The French, as part of their opposition to Diem, had supplied arms to the Cao Dai, Hoa Hao, and Binh Xuyen; but by 1956, with American aid, Diem had smashed the military strength of the three sects. Their followers, numbering about a quarter of the total population, were resentful, but remained active in a less military context.

Out of the maze of political aims, cultural diffusion, and varied religious beliefs that form the background to twentieth-century Vietnam, four principal religious groups emerged to play a significant part in more recent years: the Buddhists, the Roman Catholic Church, the Cao Dai, and the Hoa Hao.

The Cao Dai

The Cao Dai sect arose from a séance communication received by Ngo Van Chieu (1878–1926), an administrator for the French in Cochin China, in 1919. In 1926 the sect was formally organized by a wealthy compatriot and Mandarin, Le Van Trung (d. 1935). Cao Dai means 'Supreme Palace' or 'High Altar', and denotes the name of the supreme God.

Strikingly syncretistic, Cao Dai is also known as 'The Third Amnesty' of God. It was preceded by a first (Eastern) amnesty with Buddha and Lao-tzu, and a second (Western) amnesty with Moses and Jesus Christ. Cao Dai is the third and unsurpassable manifestation of God in the historical process of revelation; it requires no human representatives – God communicates directly through trance to certain devotees. In its characteristic hierarchical structure, it follows the pattern of the Roman Catholic Church, with its own pope dwelling in a village outside Tan Ninh city, near Saigon, where an ornate cathedral was built in 1937, at the foot of a high mountain. Its dignitaries include a full ranking-list of priests, bishops, and cardinals.

In addition to Catholicism and Buddhism, Cao Dai combines Confucianism, Taoism, and traditional cults of spirits and ancestors. Spiritualistic elements have a striking importance, especially contacts with the dead. Amongst a host of additional figures revered in its pantheon are Victor Hugo, Sun Yat Sen, Joan of Arc, Louis Pasteur, and Jean Decoux, the French Admiral of World War II who administered Vietnam for the Japanese. Its breadth thus appeals to the integrated view of peasant peoples; entire village communities have become its followers. The wealthy Le Van Trung had, like Buddha, renounced the luxurious life; but for villagers to whom poverty is nothing new, it is the magical elements that prove attractive.

The ethic of Cao Dai is based on the underlying concept of the transmigration of souls. Cao Dai revived traditional Buddhist rules regarding vegetarianism, attitudes towards animals, and rules for social behaviour. Fraternity and charity, however, are much stronger than in Buddhist ethics and practice. There is also a strongly marked temple cult, with numerous rites. Prayers, incense offerings, meditation, and exorcisms are of great importance. Female celebrants are permitted, and matrilineal descent is important.

The religious symbol of the community is Cao Dai's eye over the globe. Its initially rapid expansion led to struggles for leadership. Despite splitting into several sects, Cao Dai has continued to grow, and its numbers are claimed to be more than 5 million.

The Hoa Hao

This neo-Buddhist sect was started by Huynh Phu So, in the village of Hoa Hao, Vietnam, near the Cambodian border. Born in 1919, he was the son of a leading Roman Catholic peasant in the local community, and received religious training as a young man, in the hope of improving his poor health. In 1939 he experienced a violent nervous spasm, from which he emerged, not only cured, but with great power to preach and teach a new religion. Claiming to be the incarnation of several past heroes, he set this religion on a supposedly ancient foundation, which also indicated a political role for himself and his followers. He combined a revised form of Buddhist rituals with a teaching that no intermediary or

holy place is necessary for direct prayer to the Almighty.

There are four main precepts in his sect's teaching:

- honour for one's parents
- love of one's country
- respect for his interpretation of Buddhism
- love towards one's fellows

Not in temples, but in teaching-centres spread over former South Vietnam, his teachings were communicated in forms attractive to the peasant population. They sometimes had nationalistic overtones, and strangely predicted the coming of Americans two decades ahead of their arrival. Viewed in the 1940s as a 'living Buddha', his reputation rapidly drew followers to the sect. The French, however, saw him as a focus of political unrest, detained him in a psychiatric hospital, and later under house arrest. This enhanced his reputation, and from his home he taught many groups of pilgrims. A few days before a French plan to exile him to Laos could be put into action, his followers, aided by Japanese secret police, moved him to Saigon, where he was kept out of French hands.

Later it became obvious that the various nationalist movements, including Cao Dai and Hoa Hao, would each seek supremacy in the power struggle. By the late 1960s, increasingly disillusioned nationalist urban intellectuals joined the Hoa peasants' religious movement, though it remained fundamentally of rural appeal. By the time Huynh Phu So was murdered by Communists in April 1947, sub-sects had arisen which were far more active and united within themselves than were the sub-sects in the Cao Dai. The new sub-sects rejected the bribery and betrayal that discredited some Cao Dai leaders – who also suffered disunity and decline after the death of their pope in 1959. The vigorous teaching activities of Hoa Hao continued to appeal to the large rural population in the Mekong Delta, and the sect has remained a powerful force in southern Vietnam.

Barbara Boal

I AM A BUDDHIST

I was born in Brisbane, Australia, into a Roman Catholic family, and have Japanese, Irish, and English ancestry. For seventeen years I strove to be a good Catholic boy, until the time of the Vietnam War. All the Christian religious teaching I had received included as a central premise the commandment, 'Thou shall not kill.' I was therefore confused when I learned that Australia had introduced conscription for seventeen-year-old boys. This seemed to me to be hypocrisy and made me question the religion I had taken for granted. Eventually, I decided to explore my Japanese heritage.

I had already become interested in the martial arts of judo and karate. However, as I pursued my interest, I learnt that *karate* means 'empty hand' and *judo* means 'the gentle way'; that it is not violence and coercion that lead to success, but rather becoming so developed and aware that one cannot be hurt. However, much training is required to remain focused and alert. There is a saying concerning being attacked by a sword, 'The beginner can only see where the sword is, and cannot move. The master sees everywhere that the sword is not, and quietly moves there.'

Later I discovered the calm, smiling, accepting faces of the Buddha statues, which attracted me strongly. Here, in front of them, was a place where I could sit, and no one was going to criticize me; where I could let my guard down and just be a boy – relaxed and happy. Over the years, the Buddha faces became more real, as I began to

meet Buddhist monks and nuns, people who could explain in great detail why and how they looked so peaceful. In essence, it was because they had given up worrying. 'If something can be done, then do it. Do not worry. If something cannot be done, then it cannot be done. Do not worry.'

This is one of the most valuable things I have discovered as a Buddhist. It is always possible to do something useful in every situation. No matter how difficult or impossible something might seem, there is always an explanation, and always something to do next. For example, if I fail at a task and feel awful, Buddhist teaching instructs me to examine who I think I am. Am I just a collection of other people's judgments, good or bad? Or do I truly have a reality and an essence that is already complete and whole, yet is at the same time developing with everything – good or bad – that I do? This deep understanding helps me to move forward in life. If suddenly there is a mountain in front of me – whether literally or figuratively – I can either sit down defeated or start climbing upwards step by step. It is only by climbing a mountain that one becomes a good mountain climber. The same is true of every human situation. I can only become a more compassionate person by acting compassionately, a good leader by leading well, a good follower by learning to give loyalty to those who have been appointed to lead.

My Buddhist teacher tells me I must learn to love problems like chocolate! He means that problems provide opportunities to develop the wisdom to see the best way forward in every situation. Although the experience of happiness should be fully enjoyed, it is impermanent and constantly changing – just like problems. Nothing lasts forever.

After many years, I have learnt that, if my heart and my mind are truly in a compassionately wise state, the results will usually be effective and useful to myself and other people. To this end, I start each day with prayers and readings from the Buddhist lineage that I follow – the Tibetan Gelugpa lineage of His Holiness the Dalai Lama. I try, as my teacher advises, to sit in formal meditation for at least forty-five minutes each day. In this way, I can set my motivation and focus for the coming day, which on a 'normal' day is full of competing demands on my time, energy, and attention. Although I have a formal time of meditation, I seek to stay in a 'meditative state of mind' all day, which is the goal of all spiritual practice: to live the faith in the 'real world' and thereby show that it is alive and well.

In the evening, I briefly review what has happened during the day, and determine to try to be even more mindful the following day. Also, I pray that the Buddhas and gurus will watch over me throughout the night, and teach me in my dreams. This is a way of reaching through the limited conceptual mind into the core being of who I really am, and why I am really here – not the collection of public facades that I have to wear for my various roles and positions.

There are four special days of the Buddhist year on which I fast:

1. *Wesak*,
2. The Descent to teach in this world,
3. The day of the Buddha's first teaching – the Four Noble Truths,
4. Tibetan New Year.

I also try to fast on all full moon days – many Buddhists still use a lunar calendar. During the two weeks when the moon is waning, I practise reducing my negative activities; and in the two weeks of the waxing moon, I practise developing my positive qualities.

Over Christmas, I often go on a retreat and fast for forty-eight hours, drinking just a little fruit juice or black tea. I find it relatively easy, especially if I do it in a Buddhist centre, with no television, radio, or music to distract me. I am not a strict vegetarian, although some Buddhists are. As one who follows a Tibetan tradition, I am not required to be. The Tibetans, because of their environment, are not vegetarian: not many crops grow above the snow line, and yak meat is very warming in a stew. That said, the overall emphasis in Buddhism is always to try to reduce harm with every thought, word and deed.

Every week I go to my local temple to hear my teacher discuss his views on the scriptures and how to apply them in modern life. This keeps me in touch with 'real reality', rather than the reality of the newspapers and television.

Paul Seto

CHAPTER 13

Buddhism in the Modern World

What can Buddhism offer to the contemporary world? In what ways is it challenging society? In what ways is it reinforcing the traditional? To answer these questions it is first necessary to look at some of the forces that have influenced the development of Buddhism in the last two hundred years.

EUROPEAN COLONIALISM

Sri Lanka (Ceylon) was the first predominantly Buddhist country to be affected by European colonialism. When the British occupied Colombo in 1796, Sri Lanka had already known two colonial powers: the Portuguese and the Dutch, though both ruled only part of the island. The British brought the whole under foreign rule, by bringing down the previously independent Kandyan Kingdom in 1815. Myanmar (Burma) was the second Buddhist country to be affected by European colonialism. In 1795, the Burmese authorities allowed a British Resident in Yangon (Rangoon). Three Anglo-Burmese wars followed, until in 1885 all of Myanmar came under British rule. Independence for both Sri Lanka and Myanmar came in 1948. Cambodia, Laos and Vietnam were the third Buddhist areas, coming under French rule. For Cambodia, the process began in 1864, and by the 1890s the French had almost complete control over the internal running of the country. Significant also was Western penetration into China: between 1839 and 1865 the West, through military action and forced treaties, gained rights of residence and, in some parts of the country, jurisdiction.

This imperialistic movement affected Buddhism in two main ways. Firstly, Western visitors to these countries started to study Buddhism and interpret it to the West, working in tandem with European-based orientalists. In the early years of the nineteenth century, some drew on oral sources in Asia, but, as the century progressed, the texts took precedence, leading to an increasingly textualized interpretation of Buddhism in the West. Secondly, Asian Buddhism itself underwent revival, as it attempted to resist the Christian missionary activity that accompanied colonialism. In Sri Lanka, for instance, archival records suggest that Buddhists at first sought coexistence with Christians; they were willing to procure Buddhist texts for them and teach them the language of the texts, Pali. When they discovered, however, that the missionaries would use their knowledge to undermine Buddhism, hospitality turned to confrontation, and to the development of 'Protestant Buddhism' – a form of Buddhism that both 'protested' against Christianity and borrowed elements from it, from the Young Man's Buddhist Association and hymns to Protestant Christianity's emphasis on texts and devaluing of ritual. Myanmar witnessed a similar revivalist development, influenced by Sri Lanka, and in both countries revival movements and independence movements gave strength to each other. At the beginning of the twentieth century, Chinese Buddhism also underwent revival, again in response to the impact of the West, although its impact was lessened by the growth of secular ideologies.

SECULAR IDEOLOGIES AND AUTHORITARIANISM

In the middle years of the twentieth century, Buddhism in Cambodia, China, Korea, Laos, Tibet, and Vietnam was adversely affected by secular ideologies, Communism in particular. Communist leaders in China, after the establishment of the Chinese People's Republic in 1949,

Buddhist prayer flags on the mountainside, Nepal.

simply expected Buddhism to die away. When it did not, particularly from 1966–76, the years of the Cultural Revolution, there were violent attacks on Buddhist leaders and religious buildings.

It was the British withdrawal from India that gave Communist China the opportunity to invade Tibet. The process began in 1950 and culminated in 1959, when China imposed direct rule on the country and the Dalai Lama fled. Systematic suppression of Tibet's Buddhist heritage followed: the looting of monasteries; the destruction of libraries and religious images; the execution of some monks; and the torture and imprisonment of others. In the late 1970s, there was some relaxation of this policy, leading to a limited renewal of Buddhism in the country.

Cambodia gained its independence from the French in 1953. In 1975, Phnom Penh fell to the Khmer Rouge under Saloth Sar (Pol Pot, 1925–98). Although before victory the Khmer Rouge had seemed to praise Buddhism, after 1975 Buddhism was systematically dismantled, together with everything else that evoked Cambodia's former culture. Almost all Buddhist temples were razed, Buddhist monks were killed or given degrading labour, and Buddhist libraries gutted. In the Buddhist Institute in Phnom Penh, 40,000 documents were destroyed. When the Vietnamese defeated Pol Pot in 1979, the country was in ruins, and there was only a handful of Buddhist monks left.

Since 1979, Cambodia has painstakingly — and in the context of ongoing violence and war — attempted to rebuild its Buddhist heritage, gaining help from countries such as Sri Lanka, Japan, and Germany. The first priority was to rebuild the temples, after which came teachers and books. In 1992, the Buddhist Institute was re-opened. A deeper challenge than any of these has been to spark an interest in spiritual values in those Cambodians who had only known violence.

BUDDHISM ENTERS THE WEST

One consequence of China's invasion of Tibet was that thousands of Tibetans fled the country. Most went to India, Nepal, and Bhutan, but some travelled to Europe and America, internationalizing the Tibetan story, and spreading Tibetan forms of Buddhism. For instance in 1967 two Tibetans — Chogyam Trungpa Tulku Rinpoche (1939–87) and Dr Akong Tulku Rinpoche (b. 1939) — founded Kagyu Samye Ling monastery, near Eskdalemuir, southern Scotland, which has now become the largest Tibetan Buddhist centre in Europe, attracting numerous Westerners, a good number of whom have become monks and nuns.

Tibetan Buddhism, however, was not the first form of Buddhism to enter the West. In the nineteenth century, Buddhists came to British universities from countries such as Sri Lanka and Myanmar. Then, in 1893, the Anagarika Dharmapala (1864–1933), a key figure in the Buddhist Revival in Sri Lanka, visited Britain — although his principal goal was to attend the World's Parliament of Religions in Chicago — returning in 1896 and 1907. The first formal Buddhist mission to Britain, however, came from Myanmar in 1908, led by the second British person to become a Buddhist monk, Venerable Ananda Metteyya (Allan Bennett, 1872–1923), who was then living in Myanmar. The Buddhist Society of Great Britain and Northern Ireland was formed to welcome him. Allan Bennett had come to Buddhism through theosophy, and through Edwin Arnold's poem on the Buddha, *The Light of Asia*, published in 1879. This poem's presentation of the Buddha as compassionate hero drew on both Theravada and Mahayana textual sources and attracted countless readers.

The history of Buddhism in Britain and the West between 1908 and 1959 is a complex one. In 1924, the work of the Buddhist Society of Great Britain and Northern Ireland was taken over by a lawyer, Christmas Humphreys (1901–83), who combined it with a Buddhist centre he had started within the Theosophical Society, to form the Buddhist Lodge. In 1943 this was renamed The Buddhist Society, London, which continues today as the Buddhist Society. One of the inspirations for Christmas Humphreys was Daisetz Teitaro Suzuki (1870–1966), the Japanese Zen master who did more than any other person to bring Zen Buddhism to laypeople in the West. As a young man, he lived in La Salle, Illinois, but in 1921 became Professor of Buddhist Philosophy at Otani University, Tokyo. Following World War II, he resumed contact with the West, influencing a generation of Westerners, and producing more than thirty volumes on Buddhism and Zen in English.

Almost all schools of Buddhism are now present in the West, and new Buddhist organizations are emerging to meet the needs of Westerners. In Britain, for instance, Theravada Buddhism has a strong presence, with monasteries and educational centres catering for Buddhists from Sri Lanka, Thailand, Myanmar, and for Western converts. The Japanese Mahayana schools are represented – Zen, Pure Land, Tendai – and also newer lay movements such as Soka Gakkai, with its many Western followers, and Rissho Kosei-kai. The different Tibetan schools have also taken root, and there are movements such

Young Buddhist monks in Cambodia.

as the one founded in 1967 by the British Buddhist, Sangharakshita (Dennis Lingwood, b. 1925), the Triratna Buddhist Order, which aims to offer a Buddhism to Westerners that combines the best of all schools. Never in the history of Buddhism has one area of the world received so many forms of Buddhism within the same short time span.

Asian countries such as Thailand and Japan have been particularly affected by the internationalization of capital, and the individualism and consumerism that has followed in its wake. Since the mid-twentieth century, both countries have experienced phenomenal economic growth, which has led to an undermining of Buddhism's emphases on non-greed and community. On the other hand, new counter-cultural Buddhist voices have emerged, challenging forms of Buddhism that place individual well-being above the health of the whole community.

BUDDHISM, WAR, AND PEACE

Conditioned by forces such as those mentioned above, Buddhists are entering many contemporary debates. Their contribution falls into two broad categories: the dynamics of social engagement, and the benefits – and indeed necessity – of meditation as a way of preventing hatred, anger, and violence.

In Cambodia, after the fall of Pol Pot, in a situation of ongoing violence, a remarkable Buddhist movement, The Coalition for Peace and Reconciliation, grew up under the leadership of Maha Ghosananda (1929–2007), a monk who escaped the Pol Pot regime because he was in Thailand in 1975. During the 1990s, annual peace walks, or Pilgrimages for Truth (*Dhammayietras*), were held, passing through areas still torn by conflict. Monks and nuns, laywomen and men, took part, sometimes risking their lives as they walked through crossfire. Such costly witnesses for peace have characterized Buddhism in the modern world. However, Buddhists have not stood for non-violence in all situations.

The monk's vow

I shall eat whatever is given to me with appreciation.

From *The Monastic Code of Discipline*, Vinaya IV 189

Buddhism's nonviolent stance sets it against war in general. However, like followers of other faiths, Buddhists have struggled when this principle comes up against pressing and complex issues, and some strands of Buddhism developed a philosophy of the 'just war'. At times, this justification of war has seemed to predominate over nonviolence. For example, Japanese Buddhists aligned with – or at least did not resist – the militarization of Japan in the middle years of the twentieth century, an attitude criticized by Buddhists born later in the century, after the horror of Nagasaki and Hiroshima. In Sri Lanka, some Buddhist monks and laypeople have supported a military solution to the ethnic war that ravaged the country after 1983, arguing that defence of Buddhism is justified if it is seen to be threatened, though other Sri Lankan Buddhists have rejected this stance.

BUDDHISM AND WOMEN

In the Buddha's time, women received higher ordination and became nuns (Pali, *bhikkhunis*; Sanskrit, *bhiksunis*). This higher ordination was lost in Sri Lanka and Myanmar, and never transmitted to countries such as Tibet and Thailand. Even without higher ordination, however, women have left their families to become nuns, but have not officially been able to follow the complete *bhikkhuni* rule of discipline. This began to change after the founding in 1987 of Sakyadhita ('Daughters of the Buddha'), an international organization of Buddhist women. At Sakyadhita conferences, fully-ordained nuns from Mahayana countries such as Taiwan and Korea met 'contemporary nuns' from countries such as Sri Lanka. This eventually led to ordination ceremonies, at which nuns from countries such as Taiwan, together with sympathetic Theravada monks, ordained nuns from countries that had no higher ordination. This is a story still in process.

Restoring to all Buddhist women the opportunity to gain higher ordination is not simply about regaining lost 'rights'; it is about affirming what women can contribute to Buddhism. Whether all Buddhist women gain the option to renounce as fully-ordained nuns or not, Buddhist women are now coming together with urgency to meditate, to co-operate in joint projects, and to share their vision of a world transformed by the Buddha's teaching.

ENGAGED BUDDHISM

In 1989, the International Network of Engaged Buddhists was formed. Its founders included Sulak Sivaraksa (b. 1933), a lay Buddhist from Siam – he will not call himself Thai – and Thich Nhat Hanh (b. 1929), an exiled monk from Vietnam, who founded the Order of Interbeing in 1965. The Network asserted that Buddhism was not only about individual peace and liberation, but also about creating a better world now. Drawing on Buddhist concern for the elimination of suffering and the concept of interconnectedness, it sought to draw attention to the fact that the causes of much oppression, poverty, and suffering lay in unjust structures and the corporate greed of the rich. Engaged Buddhist movements are now found throughout the world. The members of the Amida Trust in Britain, for instance, draw inspiration from the Pure Land Tradition of Japan – which emphasizes that rebirth in the 'Pure Land', from where it will be easy to attain *nirvana*, is possible through relying on the compassion of the Buddha Amitabha – but direct this towards working for a 'Pure Land' here and now, a task they link with the original message of the Buddha.

Engaged Buddhists insist that meditation and social engagement go hand in hand, in line with the Buddha's message that we need to know how our minds and hearts work, if we are to act with wisdom rather than with greed and hatred. A growth of meditation centres catering for laypeople in Asia and the West is putting this message across strongly. In traditional Asian Buddhism, meditation practices – except for the most elementary – were linked with monastic life. Now, whether in Sri Lanka, Thailand, the USA, or Europe, meditation is becoming an important part of life for laypeople as well.

INTERFAITH RELATIONS

Although mistrust of Christianity is found in countries such as Sri Lanka, where Buddhists have experienced aggressive Christian missionary activity, many Buddhists across the world are involved in building bridges of understanding between faiths. Rissho Kosei-kai, for instance, a Japanese Buddhist lay movement started in 1938, was one of the founders of the World Conference on Religion and Peace in 1970, a pioneering international interfaith organization. In 1987 the US-based Society for Buddhist-Christian Studies was formed, and in October 1997 the European Network of Buddhist-Christian Studies.

Buddhism is changing, partly due to the interpenetration of Western and Eastern forms of Buddhism. The result is that Buddhism has become a positive, dynamic force in the world; one of the insights it can offer the world is that social engagement and compassionate action must go hand in hand with work on self, the work of meditation, the work of wisdom.

ELIZABETH J. HARRIS

QUESTIONS

1. Why is human experience so important for a follower of Buddhism?

2. Explain how the Four Noble Truths help Buddhists attain *nirvana*.

3. What is Mahayana Buddhism?

4. What is the difference between Theravada and Mahayana Buddhism, and why are they not directly comparable?

5. Why did Sanskrit become so important in Buddhism?

6. What is Tantric Buddhism and why is it regarded as controversial?

7. Why is abstention so important in Buddhist morality?

8. What is Cao Dai, and how does it differ from other Buddhist traditions?

9. Explain the role of meditation in Buddhism.

10. Explain some of the different ways that Buddhism has been affected by encounters with the West.

FURTHER READING

Blomfield, Vishvapani, *Gautama Buddha: The Life and Times of the Awakened One*. London: Quercus, 2011.

Bui, Hum Dac, and Beck, Ngasha, *Cao Dai: Faith of Unity*. Fayetteville, AR: Emerald Wave, 2000.

Dalai Lama, *How to Practice: The Way to a Meaningful Life*. Trans. and ed. Jeffrey Hopkins. New York: Pocket Books, 2002.

Fisher, Robert E., *Buddhist Art and Architecture*. London: Thames & Hudson, 2002.

Gunaratana, Bhante H., *Mindfulness in Plain English*. Boston: Wisdom Publications, 2002.

Harvey, P., An Introduction to Buddhism: Teachings, History and Practices. Cambridge: Cambridge University Press, 1990.

Lopez, Donald S. Jr., *The Story of Buddhism: A Concise Guide to its History and Teachings*. New York: HarperCollins, 2002.

Queen, Christopher S., and King, Sallie B, eds., *Engaged Buddhism: Liberation Movements in Asia*. Albany: State University of New York Press, 1996.

Thich Nhat Hanh, *The Heart of the Buddha's Teaching*. New York: Broadway, 1999.

Williams, Paul, *Buddhist Thought: A Complete Introduction to the Indian Tradition*. New York, Routledge, 2000.

GALLERY

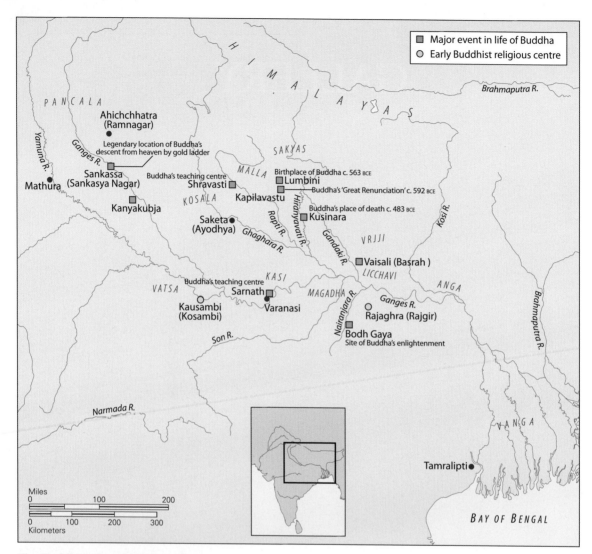

The Buddhist Heartland

A BRIEF INTRODUCTION TO BUDDHISM

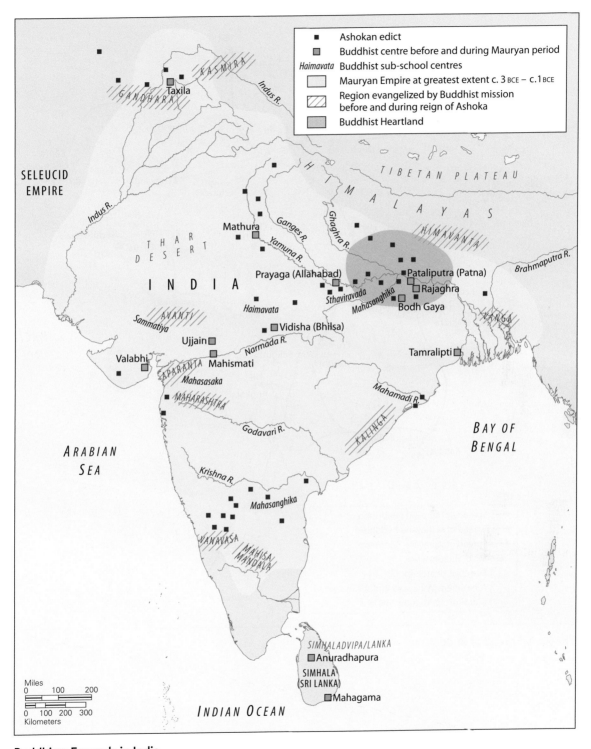

Legend:

- ■ Ashokan edict
- ■ Buddhist centre before and during Mauryan period
- *Haimavata* Buddhist sub-school centres
- ☐ Mauryan Empire at greatest extent c. 3 BCE – c.1 BCE
- ⧅ Region evangelized by Buddhist mission before and during reign of Ashoka
- ▨ Buddhist Heartland

SELEUCID EMPIRE

KASMIRA

GANDHARA

Indus R.

Taxila

TIBETAN PLATEAU

H I M A L A Y A S

Indus R.

THAR DESERT

Mathura

Ganges R.

Yamuna R.

Ghaghra R.

HIMAVANTA

Brahmaputra R.

I N D I A

Prayaga (Allahabad)

Pataliputra (Patna)

Rajaghra

Sthaviravada

Mahasanghika

Bodh Gaya

VANGA

Haimavata

AVANTI

Sammatiya

Vidisha (Bhilṣa)

Ujjain

Narmada R.

Tamralipti

Valabhi

APARANTA

Mahismati

Mahasasaka

MAHARASHTRA

Mahamadi R.

Godavari R.

KALINGA

ARABIAN SEA

Krishna R.

Mahasanghika

BAY OF BENGAL

VANAVASA

MAHISA MANDALA

SIMHALADVIPA/LANKA

Anuradhapura

SIMHALA (SRI LANKA)

INDIAN OCEAN

Mahagama

Miles
0   100   200

0   100 200 300
Kilometers

Buddhism Expands in India

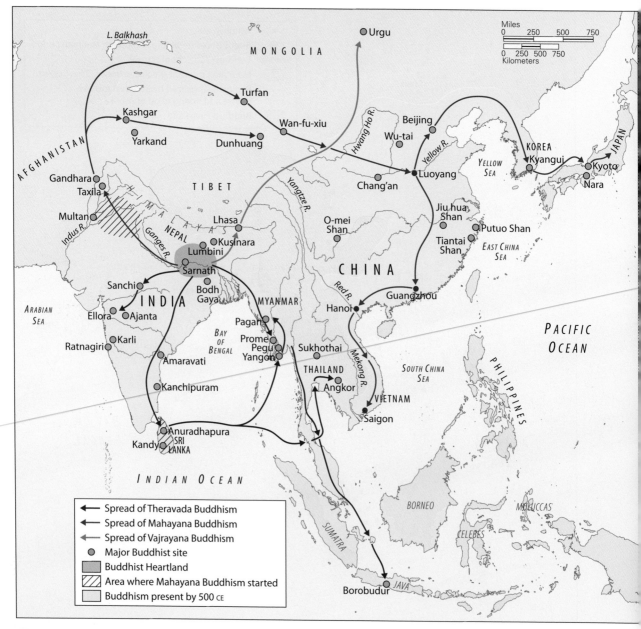

The Early Spread of Buddhism

A BRIEF INTRODUCTION TO BUDDHISM

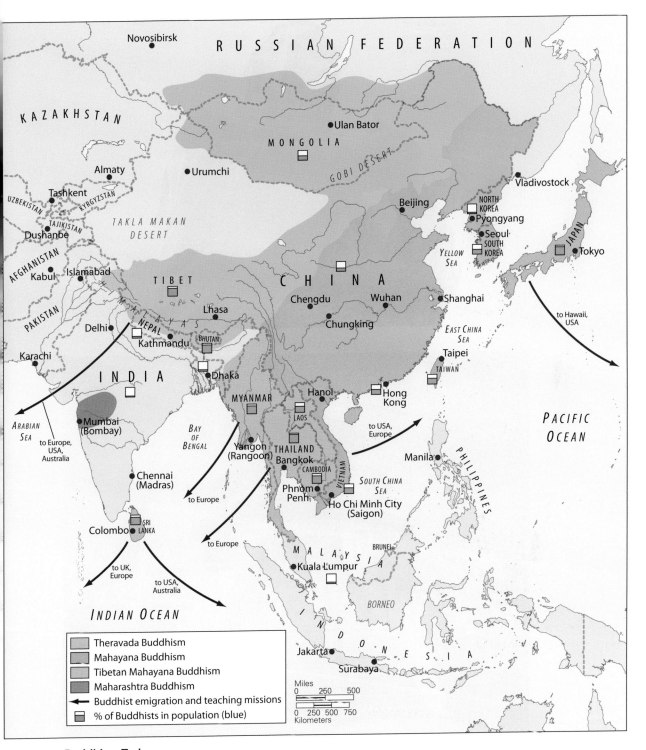

Buddhism Today

Stone statue of Confucius from a Chinese temple.

The Hall of Prayer in the Taoist Temple of Heaven, Beijing, China.

A BRIEF INTRODUCTION TO BUDDHISM

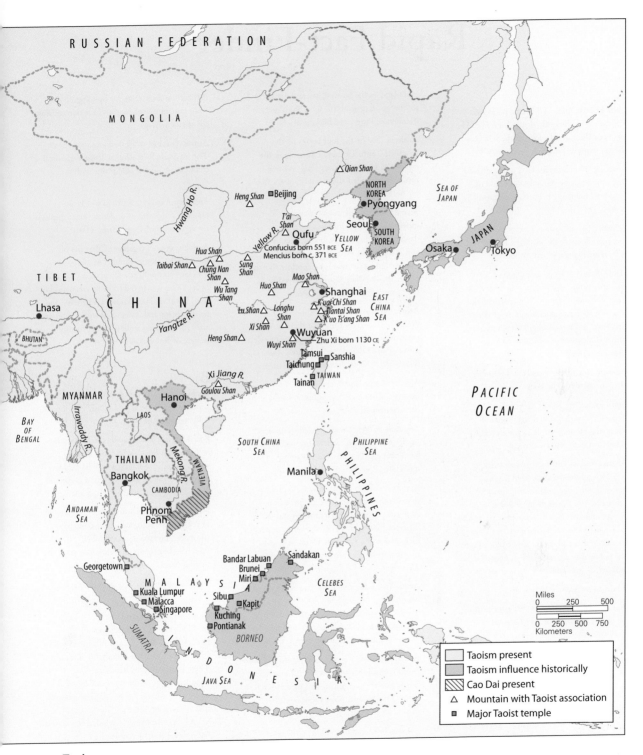

RUSSIAN FEDERATION

MONGOLIA

△ Qian Shan

NORTH
KOREA
● Pyongyang

Heng Shan ■Beijing
△

Hwang Ho R.

T'ai
Shan
△ Qufu
Confucius born 551 BCE
Mencius born c. 371 BCE

Yellow R.

YELLOW
SEA

Seoul ■
SOUTH
KOREA

SEA OF
JAPAN

JAPAN
Osaka ● Tokyo

Hua Shan
△

TIBET

Taibai Shan △ △ Chung Nan
Shan

Sung
Shan △

Wu Tang
Shan

Huo Shan
△

Mao Shan
△

CHINA

● Shanghai

● Lhasa

Lu Shan Longhu
△ Shan
△

Yangtze R.

Xi Shan
△

K'uai Chi Shan
△ Tiantai Shan
△ K'uo Ts'ang Shan

EAST
CHINA
SEA

BHUTAN

Heng Shan △

Wuyi Shan
△

● Wuyuan
Zhu Xi born 1130 CE

Tamsui
■
Taichung ■ Sanshia

MYANMAR

Xi Jiang R.

Goulou Shan
△

Hanoi ●

TAIWAN
Tainan ●

LAOS

PACIFIC
OCEAN

BAY
OF
BENGAL

Irrawaddy R.

THAILAND

Bangkok ●

Mekong R.

VIETNAM

CAMBODIA

Phnom
Penh ●

SOUTH CHINA
SEA

PHILIPPINE
SEA

ANDAMAN
SEA

Manila ●

PHILIPPINES

Bandar Labuan
Brunei ■
Miri ■

Sandakan
■

Georgetown ■

MALAYSIA

Kuala Lumpur ■
Malacca ■
Singapore ■

Sibu
■

Kapit
■

CELEBES
SEA

Kuching ■
Pontianak ■

BORNEO

SUMATRA

INDONESIA

JAVA SEA

Miles
0   250   500

0   250   500 750
Kilometers

☐ Taoism present
▨ Taoism influence historically
▧ Cao Dai present
△ Mountain with Taoist association
■ Major Taoist temple

Taoism

Rapid Fact-Finder

A

Abhidhamma Pitaka Theravada Buddhist scripture on techniques of mind-training. The aim is to eliminate the idea of the self. It is the key work of Buddhist psychology.

Absolute, The Term for God or the divine often preferred by those who conceive of God predominantly in abstract or impersonal terms.

Advaita ('non-dualism') The monist (*see* monism) doctrine of Shankara, that all reality is fundamentally one and divine.

Æsir Plural of '*as*', meaning 'god'. The collective noun used in Norse literature for the pantheon of deities. More particularly, it is used of a particular majority group that share a common origin, which includes principal deities such as Odin, Thor, and Tyr. (See also Vanir.)

Afterlife Any form of conscious existence after the death of the body.

Agni Indian fire god of Vedic times (*see* Vedas). As sacrificial fire, Agni mediates between gods and people and is especially concerned with order and ritual.

Ahimsa Indian virtue of non-violence. It usually applies to abstention from harming any living creature and hence to vegetarianism. The doctrine was developed in Jainism, Buddhism, and some Hindu sects. In Jain belief violence carries severe penalties of karma. Mahatma Gandhi applied the idea to the political struggles of the oppressed in his practice of non-violent non-cooperation.

Ahriman *see* Angra Mainyu.

Almsgiving The giving of free gifts, usually of money, to the poor. In Theravada Buddhism the lay community is linked to the sangha by their provision of food for the monks, which is collected on a daily almsround.

Amida *see* Amitabha.

Amitabha ('infinite light') Celestial Buddha worshipped in China and Japan (where his name is Amida). He is believed to live in a 'pure land' in the far west where those faithful to him go after death (*see* Jodo Shinshu; Nembutsu; Pure Land Buddhism).

Analects One of the four books of the so-called Confucian canon. It contains the essence of Confucius's teaching and was probably compiled about seventy years after his death.

Ananda One of the most prominent members of the Buddha's sangha. Traditionally he was the Buddha's cousin and many of the sayings are addressed to him, including the words of comfort shortly before the Buddha's death. He helped to fix the canon of Buddhist scripture.

Anatta/Anatman Meaning 'not-self', a Buddhist term indicating that there is no permanent self or ego. All beings are merely a series of mental and physical states. *Anatta* is one of the three characteristics of existence.

Anicca/Anitya Buddhist term for the impermanence and changeability which characterizes all existence.

Animism A term formerly used to describe pre-literary religions. It was dropped because its meaning, 'spiritism', was felt to be misleading. (*See* indigenous religions.)

Archetypes Term invented by C. G. Jung to describe the concepts held in common by different people at different times and in different places. He believed that the concept of God was the archetype of the self and that it was the object of each individual to discover it.

Aryan Word describing the Caucasian people who invaded India around 2000 BCE and who gradually imposed their language and culture upon the earlier inhabitants. Related peoples settled in Iran and Mesopotamia.

Asceticism Austere practices designed to lead to the control of the body and the senses. These may include fasting and meditation, the renunciation of possessions, and the pursuit of solitude.

Ashram In Indian religion, a hermitage or monastery. It has come to denote a communal house for devotees of a guru.

It functions as a centre for building up the commitment of believers and for transmitting the guru's message.

Atman Sanskrit word meaning soul or self. The Upanishads teach that *atman* is identical to brahman, i.e. the soul is one with the divine.

Austerity Ascetic practice in which one exercises self-restraint or denial, for example, the restriction of food during a fast.

Avalokiteshvara ('regarder of the cries of the earth') Celestial Buddha worshipped by Tibetans and in Korea, Japan, and China. The Dalai Lama is believed to be an emanation of him. This Buddha is known under male and female forms and is depicted with a thousand arms symbolizing endless labour for the welfare of humankind.

B

Bodhi In various schools of Buddhism, 'awakening', or 'perfect wisdom', or 'supreme enlightenment' (I).

Bodhidharma Traditionally the first teacher of Ch'an Buddhism who moved from southern India to China in c. 520 CE. He introduced the methods of sharp questioning and paradox found today in Japanese Zen.

Bodhisattva In Mahayana Buddhism a saint or semi-divine being who has voluntarily renounced nirvana in order to help others to salvation. In popular devotion *bodhisattvas* are worshipped as symbols of compassion.

Bon/Bön A branch of Tibetan Vajrayana.

Buddha ('the one who has awakened'/'enlightened one')
(I) Siddhartha Guatama, a sage of the Shakya tribe who lived in India in around the sixth century BCE, the founder of Buddhism. There is little doubt that there was a historical figure at the source of Buddhism, though some branches of Mahayana regard this as unimportant.
(2) Any human being or celestial figure who has reached enlightenment (I).

Buddhaghosa Buddhist writer of the fifth century CE who wrote many commentaries on the scriptures and one original work, *The Path of Purification*. The Burmese believe he was a native of Myanmar (Burma) but other traditions hold that he was an Indian who worked in Sri Lanka (Ceylon).

Buddha image Representation of the Buddha used in all forms of Buddhism. The Buddha is most commonly portrayed in the lotus posture, but there are also versions of him standing or lying on one side. The various postures and position of the hands symbolize the defeat of evil, the achieving of enlightenment, the preaching of the dhamma, and the final nirvana. The images are psychological aids rather than objects of worship, though in Mahayana Buddhism they act as a focus for devotion.

Buddhism The religion which developed from the teaching of the Buddha and which spread from India into south-east Asia, later expanding into northern Asia, China and Japan. The two principal divisions are the Theravada (Hinayana) and the Mahayana. Special features are found in Tibetan Buddhism, also known as Vajrayana.

Butsudan A Japanese domestic altar to the Buddha which contains images or objects of worship and memorial tablets to ancestors. There may be lights, flowers, and incense and it is the focus of daily prayer chanting and the offering of food and drink.

C

Cao Dai Religious and political movement which started in southern Vietnam around 1920. It is sometimes called the 'Third Amnesty'. Firmly nationalistic, its teachings are a mixture of Buddhism and Taoism.

Chant Type of singing in which many syllables are sung on a single note or a repeated short musical phrase. Many religions use chanting in worship. Buddhists and others their own sacred scriptures. The repetitive nature of chanting can aid meditation.

Characteristics of existence In the Buddha's teaching all existence is marked by the three characteristics: anatta; anicca; dukkha.

Chorten *see* Stupa.

Civil religion Religion as a system of beliefs, symbols, and practices which legitimate the authority of a society's institutions and bind people together in the public sphere.

Cosmology (1) The study of the nature of the cosmos. (2) In religion, cosmologies concern the relationship between the divine and the natural world. This relationship is usually described in myths or stories of how God or the gods had brought the world, humanity, and particular peoples into existence and how they continue to relate to them. Cosmologies form the frameworks within which reality is interpreted.

Creation myth A story that explains the divine origins of a particular people, a place or the whole world. In some indigenous religions and ancient religions it is ritually re-enacted at the beginning of each year.

D

Dalai Lama Former religious and secular leader of Tibet, widely held to be the reincarnation of Avalokiteshvara. Since the Chinese takeover of Tibet the Dalai Lama has lived in India. He is still regarded as the spiritual leader of Tibetan Buddhists. (*See also* lama.)

Devadatta Cousin of the Buddha, and one of his earliest disciples. In some texts he is in conflict with the Buddha and leads a schismatic movement. He was condemned to a period in hell for his misdeeds.

Dhamma The teaching of the Buddha – his analysis of existence expressed in the Four Noble Truths and his cure as outlined in the Noble Eightfold Path. Dhamma is sometimes represented as an eight-spoked wheel. (*See also* dharma.)

Dhammapada One of the best-known texts of the Pali Canon expounding the essence of Theravada Buddhist teachings. It encourages Buddhist disciples to achieve their own salvation, relying on no external saviour or authority.

Dharma The teaching of the Buddha (*see* dhamma).

Divinities Name given to minor gods or spirits in indigenous religions who rule over an area of the world or some human activity – e.g. storms, war, farming, marriage. Divinities are usually worshipped formally with special rituals and festivals.

Doctrine A religious teaching or belief which is taught and upheld within a particular religious community.

Dravidian Word describing the pre-Aryan civilization based in the Indus valley. It was overturned by Aryan invaders around 2000 BCE. Today Dravidian peoples inhabit southern India.

Dukkha Buddhist term for unsatisfactoriness or suffering. Birth, illness, decay, death, and rebirth are symptoms of a restless and continuous 'coming-to-be' which marks all existence as *dukkha*.

E

Enlightenment (1) Full spiritual awakening. (2) In Buddhism, the realization of the truth of all existence which was achieved by the Buddha in his meditation at Bodh Gaya. Enlightenment or final enlightenment also refers to the passing into nirvana of anyone who follows the Buddha's way and attains release from the cycle of birth and rebirth. (*See also* bodhi.)

Esoteric Word meaning 'inner', suggesting something (e.g. a knowledge or a teaching) that is available only for the specially initiated and secret from outsiders and perhaps even from ordinary believers.

F

Faith Attitude of belief, in trust and commitment to a divine being or a religious teaching. It can also refer to the beliefs of a religion, 'the faith', which is passed on from teachers to believers.

Fasting Total or partial abstinence from food, undertaken as a religious discipline. In indigenous religions it is often a preparation for a ceremony of initiation. It is also more generally used as a means of gaining clarity of vision and mystical insight.

Feng Shui Literally translated as 'wind' and 'water', it is the Chinese art of living in harmony with one's environment in order to ensure happiness and prosperity. It emerged during the Han dynasty (206 BCE– 220 CE) and, by the twelfth century, had been developing into the quasi-science of geomancy. Based on the notion that there are five basic elements (earth, fire, metal, water, wood) and two fundamental forces (yin and yang), it studies the interaction between these in order to discover the most auspicious and powerful places. Hence, for example, feng shui is used to make wise decisions about the location of buildings, furniture, and gardens, all of which are believed to contribute to human well-being.

Fire sermon One of the Buddha's most famous sermons traditionally preached at Gaya to 1000 fire-worshipping ascetics, in which he explained that all that exists is burning with lust, anger, and ignorance.

Five precepts Ethical restraints for Buddhists, who are to refrain from: taking life, stealing, wrong sexual relations, wrong use of speech, drugs and intoxicants.

Four noble truths The Buddha's analysis of the problem of existence – a four-stage summary of his teaching:
(1) all that exists is unsatisfactory;
(2) the cause of unsatisfactoriness (dukkha) is craving (tanha);
(3) unsatisfactoriness ends when craving ends; (4) craving can be ended by practising the Noble Eightfold Path.

G

Gautama/Gotama Family name of the Buddha. Legend depicts him as a great prince born into a royal household. Modern scholars think that his father was probably the head of an aristocratic family living in the town of Kapilavastu.

God (1) The creator and sustainer of the universe; the absolute being on whom all that is depends. (2) A being with divine power and attributes; a deity, a major Divinity.

Goddess (1) Female form of god. (2) The supreme being conceived as female as in some modern Pagan religious movements. Worshippers of the Goddess claim that they are continuing the ancient religion of the Mother Goddess who was a personification of nature.

Gotama *see* **Gautama**.

H

Hell Realm where the wicked go after death. Religious teachings differ over whether this punishment is reformatory or eternal. Even religions which have a doctrine of reincarnation, such as Buddhism and Hinduism, include teachings about hells (although the belief in reincarnation makes them quite different from the teachings of Christianity and Islam).

Hinayana ('lesser vehicle') Buddhist term used to indicate the doctrine of salvation for oneself alone, in contrast to Mahayana. Most Buddhists of south-east Asia prefer the term Theravada to describe this school of Buddhism.

Holiness The sacred power, strangeness, and otherness of the divine.

Honen (1133–1212 CE) Japanese teacher of Pure Land Buddhism. He taught that repetition of the word nembutsu is all that is necessary for salvation. He is said to have recited it 60,000 times a day.

Hui Yuan *see* **Pure Land Buddhism**.

I

Incense Sweet-smelling smoke used in worship, made by burning certain aromatic substances.

Indigenous religions The preferred term for religions which are sometimes referred to as 'primal', 'tribal', 'traditional', 'primitive', and 'non-/pre-literate' religions. That said, indigenous religions are often developments of the traditional religions of tribal and aboriginal cultures. The problem with the earlier terminology was that it suggested simple, undeveloped, non-progressive, and archaic belief systems. Contemporary indigenous religions include Native American religion and Australian Aboriginal religion.

Initiation Ceremony marking coming of age, or entry into adult membership of a community. It is also used of the secret ceremonies surrounding membership of the mystery religions. (*See also* confirmation; navjote; Rites of Passage; Sacred Thread Ceremony.)

International Society for Krishna Consciousness (ISKCON) Founded in 1965 by A. C.

J

Jodo Japanese name for Pure Land Buddhism.

Jodo Shinshu ('True Pure Land Sect') A refinement of Pure Land Buddhism founded by Shinran. It was characterized by the doctrine of salvation through faith alone and the abolition of the Sangha.

Jung, C. G. (Carl Gustav) (1875–1961 CE) Swiss psychiatrist who invented the theory of archetypes. He investigated the significance of myths, symbols, and dreams, and found in them evidence for a 'collective unconscious' which was at the root of religion.

K

Karma Sanskrit word for work or action. In Indian belief every action has inevitable consequences which attach themselves to the doer requiring reward or punishment. Karma is thus the moral law of cause and effect. It explains the inequalities of life as the consequences of actions in previous lives. The notion of karma probably developed among the Dravidian people of India. In Mahayana Buddhism the concept is transformed by the idea of the bodhisattva. Merit can be transferred by grace or faith, thus changing the person's karma.

Khalsa Originally the militant community of Sikhs organized by Guru Gobind Singh in 1699 CE. Now it is the society of fully committed adult members of the Sikh community. Membership is signified by the 'Five Ks': uncut hair, a comb worn in the hair, a small dagger, shorts, and an iron or steel bracelet.

Koan Technique used in Rinzai Zen to bring about satori. It is a mind-bending question given by a teacher to a pupil to help him or her break through the prison of mental concepts and achieve direct awareness of reality.

Kuan-yin Chinese name for the great bodhisattva Avalokiteshvara, especially when thought of in female form.

Kukai (774–835 CE) Japanese Buddhist teacher who tried to reconcile Buddhism with Shinto. He is sometimes regarded as a manifestation of the Buddha Vairocana. Some believe he exists in a deep trance from which he is able to perform miracles and that he will return one day as a saviour.

Kundalini Energy that is coiled like a serpent at the base of the spine according to Tantrism. When awakened by yoga it leaps up the spine to the brain giving an experience of union and liberation re-enacting the sexual union of Shiva and Shakti.

L

Laity (from Greek *laos*, 'people') The non-ordained members of a religious community (*see* ordination), or those with no specialist religious function.

Lama Tibetan religious leader, a title formerly applied only to abbots, but later used of any monk. Lamas have been credited with magical powers which are said to be attained through years of arduous training. Their most common feat is telepathy, but they are also reported to be able to leave their bodies at will, cover huge distances at great speed, and know the time and place of their own death. (*See also* shaman.)

Libation The ritual outpouring of drink as an offering to divinities or ancestor spirits.

Lotus Type of water lily, a Buddhist symbol of enlightenment. The roots of the lotus are buried in the earth while the flower opens out above the water.

Lotus posture Style of sitting upright and cross-legged, used as a position for meditation in Hindu and Buddhist practice.

Lotus Sutra Mahayana Buddhist scripture in the form of a sermon preached by the Buddha (I) to a vast throng of gods, demons, rulers, and cosmic powers. It contains the essence of Mahayana teachings on the eternity of the Buddha, the universal capacity for Buddhahood, and the compassion and power of the bodhisattvas. It is especially revered in Japan and is the basic scripture of the Nichiren Buddhist new religions.

M

Magic The manipulation of natural or supernatural forced by spells and rituals for good or harmful ends.

Mahayana ('large/great vehicle') The form of Buddhism practised in Nepal, China, Tibet, Korea, and Japan. Mahayana accepts more scriptures than Theravada, and has developed various forms of popular devotion based on the doctrine of the bodhisattvas.

Maitreya The Buddha-to-be, or the next Buddha to appear on earth according to Mahayana teachings. He is at present a bodhisattva awaiting his last rebirth.

Mana Polynesian word for the invisible spiritual power which permeates all things. It has been adopted as a general term in the study of indigenous religions. It is not necessarily a personal power, though it can be focused in particular individuals, places, and objects.

Mandala A visual aid in the form of a series of coloured concentric circles used in Buddhism and Hinduism. Segments of the circles portray different aspects of the Buddha's compassion. Concentration on the *mandala* enables the disciple to see himself in relation to the Buddha's compassion and thus to achieve enlightenment.

Mantra A symbolic sound causing an internal vibration which helps to concentrate the mind and aids self-realization, e.g. the repeated syllable 'om', and in Tibetan Buddhism the phrase om mani padme hum. In Hinduism the term originally referred to a few sacred verses from the Vedas. It came to be thought that they possessed spiritual power, and that repetition of them was a help to liberation. A mantra is sometimes given by a spiritual teacher to a disciple as an initiation.

Mara In Buddhism, the evil one, temptation.

Marriage, sacred A religious rite involving real or simulated sexual intercourse which represents the marriage of earth and sky in the fertilization of the soil and the growth of the crops.

Maya Legendary mother of the Buddha.

Meditation Deep and continuous reflection, practised in many religions with a variety of aims, e.g. to attain self-realization or, in theistic religions, to attain union with the divine will. Many religions teach a correct posture, method of breathing, and ordering of thoughts for meditation.

Medium One who is possessed by the spirit of a dead person or a divinity and, losing his or her individual identity, becomes the mouthpiece for the other's utterance.

Merit In Buddhism the fruit of good actions which can be devoted to the welfare of other beings. The idea develops in Mahayana, where it is believed that the bodhisattvas have acquired almost infinite supplies of merit which they can transfer to believers.

Middle Way The Buddha's description of his teaching as a mean between the extremes of sensuality and asceticism. It is designed to lead to nirvana.

Mindfulness Buddhist method of contemplative analysis. It has two uses in meditation, where it refers to the practice of observing the arising and passing away of different mental states until one arrives at detachment; in daily life, where it refers to a quality of carefulness in thought, speech, and action which prevents the accumulation of bad karma.

Ming Chinese emperor (first century CE) of the Han dynasty who, according to tradition, introduced Buddhist scriptures from north-west India. According to tradition he had a dream of a golden man, which he took to be a revelation of the Buddha.

Miracle An event which appears to defy rational explanation and is attributed to divine intervention.

Mission The outreach of a religion to the unconverted. Whereas understandings of mission vary from faith to faith, the various aims of mission usually include spiritual conversion. However, mission is often conceived more holistically and concerns, not just spiritual conversion, but the transformation of all areas of life. It addresses injustice, suffering, poverty, racism, sexism, and all forms of oppression.

Missionaries Those who propagate a religious faith among people of a different faith. Buddhism and Christianity have been the most notable missionary religions.

Moksha Sanskrit word meaning liberation from the cycle of birth, death, and rebirth. Permanent spiritual perfection experienced by an enlightened soul after the physical body has died. No further incarnations will be endured.

Monk A member of a male religious community living under vows which usually include poverty, chastity, and the wearing of a distinctive form of dress. Monastic orders are found in Christianity, Buddhism, Hinduism, and Jainism. The Buddhist monk is a member of a sangha and, additionally to the Five Precepts, vows to eat only at set times, not to handle money, use a high bed, use scent, or go to stage performances.

Monotheism The belief that there is one supreme God who contains all the attributes and characteristics of divinity.

Mystic One who seeks direct personal experience of the divine and may use prayer, meditation or various ascetic practices to concentrate the attention.

Mysticism The search for direct personal experience of the divine. There is a distinction between seeing mysticism as leading to identification with God (as is common in Hinduism) and as leading to a union with God's love and will (as in Islam, Judaism, and Christianity).

Myth A sacred story which originates and circulates within a particular community. Some aetiological myths explain puzzling physical phenomena or customs, institutions and practices whose origin in the community would otherwise be mysterious. (*See also* Creation myth.)

N

Nagarjuna (c. 150–250 CE) Mahayana Buddhist philosopher who taught that the truth of reality was void or emptiness.

Namu Myoho Renge Kyo Formula coined by Nichiren as the essential truth of the Lotus Sutra. It means 'Reverence to the wonderful truth of the *Lotus Sutra*' and it is used by a variety of sects based on Nichiren's Buddhist teachings.

Nature spirits Spirits of trees, hills, rivers, plants, and animals which are acknowledged with prayers and offerings in most indigenous religions.

Nembutsu ('Hail to the Buddha Amida') The formula of faith taught by the Japanese Buddhist teacher Honen.

Nibbana Pali word for nirvana.

Nichiren (1222–1282 CE) Japanese Buddhist reformer who taught that the Lotus Sutra contained the ultimate truth and that it could be compressed into a sacred formula: namu myoho renge kyo. He denounced all other forms of Buddhism. When the

Mongols threatened Japan he preached a fiery nationalism, urging the nation to convert to true Buddhism. His teachings have provided the inspiration for some modern Buddhist sects.

Nirvana ('going out', 'becoming cool') In Buddhism, the state when dukkha ceases because the flames of desire are no longer fuelled. It is a state of unconditioned-ness and uncompounded-ness beyond any form of known or imagined existence.

Noble Eightfold Path In Buddhism, the way to extinguish desire by adopting right views; right resolves; right speech; right action; right livelihood; right effort; right mindfulness; right concentration/meditation.

Nun A member of a religious community of women, as found in Christianity, Buddhism, hinduism, and Jainism. Nuns live under vows usually including poverty, and chastity and often the wearing of a distinctive form of dress.

O

Om mani padme hum ('the jewel in the lotus') Tibetan mantra whose six syllables are held to correspond to the six worlds of Tibetan Buddhist teaching: om, 'gods'; ma, 'anti-gods'; ni, 'humans'; pad, 'animals'; mi, 'hungry ghosts'; hum, 'hell'. Each world is present as a state of the human mind. The mantra sums up the whole of human existence and is an indispensable aid to self-realization.

Omnipotence All-powerful.

Omniscience All-knowing. Simultaneous knowledge of all things.

Ordination Rite In Buddhism the term denotes entry into the Sangha.

P

Pagan/Paganism The word 'pagan' (derived from the Latin term *pagus*, which literally means 'from the countryside' or 'rural') was first used in a general religious sense by the early Christians to describe the non-Christian gentile religions. It is now generally used to refer to a broad range of nature-venerating religious traditions.

Pagoda A Buddhist building in south-east Asia built over Buddhist relics and often characterized by a series of superimposed spires. It is an evolution of the ancient stupa.

Pali Vernacular language of northern India in the Buddha's time, and hence the language of early Buddhism and the Theravada scriptures. It is related to Sanskrit.

Pali Canon The basic Buddhist scriptures – the only scriptures valid among Theravada Buddhists. Traditionally the collection began soon after the Buddha's death when his followers met to receive the Tipitaka/ Tripitaka or 'three baskets' of his teaching. The precise wording of the canon was fixed at a council in 29 BCE.

Panchen Lama Title given to one of the leading abbots of Tibetan Buddhism, whose authority paralleled that of the Dalai Lama, though its emphasis was more on spiritual matters. The Panchen Lama was believed to be a reincarnation of Amitabha.

Pantheism The belief that all reality is in essence divine.

Pilgrimage A journey to a holy place, undertaken as a commemoration of a past event, as a celebration, or as an act of penance (*see also* hajj). The goal might be a natural feature such as a sacred river or mountain, or the location of a miracle, revelation, or theophany, or the tomb of a hero or saint.

Plato (c. 427–347 BCE) Greek philosopher and pupil of Socrates. He taught the theory of Forms or Ideas, which are eternal prototypes of the phenomena encountered in ordinary experience. Above all is the Form of the Good, which gives unity and value to all the forms. Plato also taught the immortality of the soul.

PL Kyodan ('Perfect Liberty Association') One of the new religions of Japan, founded in 1924 It is based on Shinto but accepts karma from Buddhism and teaches that the ancestors have an influence on the lives of believers. Its motto is 'life is art' and it sponsors games centres and golf clubs as well as shrines and temples.

Polytheism The belief in and worship of a variety of gods, who rule over various aspects of the world and life.

Prayer The offering of worship, requests, confessions, or other communication to God or gods publicly or privately, with or without words; often a religious obligation.

Prayer wheels Wheels and cylinders used by Buddhists in Tibet and northern India. They are inscribed with the mantra 'Om mani padme hum', the powerful effect of which is multiplied as the wheels turn.

Puja ('reverence') Refers to temple and domestic worship in Buddhism and Hinduism, and to the keeping of rites and ceremonies prescribed by the Brahmins.

Puranas A vast corpus of sacred writings (c. 350–950 CE), which include mythologies of Hindu deities and avatars of Vishnu, the origins of the cosmos, and of humanity, pilgrimage, ritual, law codes, caste obligations, and so on. There are eighteen principal Puranas, each exalting a member of the *Trimurti* (Brahma, Vishnu, Shiva). They are very important in popular Hinduism, Jainism, and Buddhism, the most popular being the *Bhagavata Purana*, which deals with Krishna's early life and encourages devotion to him (bhakti).

Pure Land Buddhism Buddhist sect founded by a Chinese monk, Hui-Yuan (334–416 CE) who was called the First Patriarch of Pure Land Buddhism. It is characterized by faith in the bodhisattva Amitabha, the creator of a 'pure land' in the west. Through faith his devotees hoped to be transported there after death.

R

Rebirth Buddhist modification of reincarnation in the light of the anatta teaching. The karmic (*see* karma) residue of one's life and actions are reclothed in the attributes and qualities acquired in the previous life. After a while this karmic 'bundle' is reborn.

Red Hats Unreformed branch of Tibetan Buddhism whose practices owe much to the former Tibetan religion of Bon, or Bön.

Religion (from Latin religare, 'to tie something tightly') A system of belief and worship, held by a community who may express its religion through shared myths, doctrines, ethical teachings, rituals, or the remembrance of special experiences.

Renunciation Giving up ownership of material possessions. In some religions, such as Buddhism, renunciation extends to psychological detachment from material possessions, including one's own body.

Rinzai Zen School of Zen which employs startling techniques (e.g. koans) to induce satori.

Rissho Kosei Kai An offshoot of the Reiyukai movement which is spreading the teachings of Nichiren Buddhism beyond the boundaries of Japan. The sect claims over 6.5 million members.

Rites of passage Religious ceremonies which mark the transition from one state of life to another. In many religions these transitional periods are felt to be dangerous and to require spiritual protection. Examples include birth rites, initiation rites, marriage rites, and funeral rites.

Ritual Religious ceremonial performed according to a set pattern of words, movements, and symbolic actions. Rituals may involve the dramatic re-enactment of ancient myths featuring gods and heroes, performed to ensure the welfare of the community.

S

Sacred Thread ceremony Initiation ceremony performed on Hindu and Buddhist boys. A sacred thread is placed around the neck indicating that the boy is one of the twice-born and has entered the first stage of life.

Sacrifice The ritual offering of animal or vegetable life to establish communion between humans and a god or gods.

Salvation In Eastern religions, release from the changing material world to identification with the absolute.

Samsara ('stream of existence') Sanskrit word which refers to the cycle of birth and death followed by rebirth as applied both to individuals and to the universe itself.

Sanctuary A place consecrated to a god, a holy place, a place of divine refuge and protection. Also, the holiest part of a sacred place or building. Historically, in some cultures, a holy place where pursued criminals or victims were guaranteed safety.

Sangha Community of Buddhist monks which started with the Buddha's first disciples. The functions of the *sangha* are to promote through its own lifestyle the best conditions for attaining individual salvation and to teach the dhamma to all people.

Satori Enlightenment in Zen Buddhism.

Scripture Writings which are believed to be divinely inspired or especially authoritative within a particular religious community.

Sect A group, usually religious (but it can be political), which has separated itself from an established tradition, claiming to teach and practise a truer form of the faith from which it has separated itself. It is, as such, often highly critical of the wider tradition which it has left.

Shakyamuni ('The wise man of the Shakyas') One of the names of the Buddha.

Shakyas Tribe to which the Buddha's family belonged. They occupied territory in the Himalayan foothills.

Shingon 'True Word' sect of Japanese Buddhism founded in the ninth century CE and characterized by a complex sacramental and magical ritual which may have been influenced by Tantrism and by indigenous Shinto practices.

Shinran (1173–1263 CE) Disciple of Honen and founder of the Japanese Buddhist sect Jodo Shinshu.

Shotoku, Prince Japanese ruler who introduced Buddhism as the state religion. During his reign (593–622 CE) he built a Buddhist academy and temple near the state capital at Nara.

Siddhartha Personal name of Gautama the Buddha.

Skandha/Khandha Term referring to the five factors which compound human personality according to Buddhist teaching. They are form, sense perception, consciousness, intellectual power, and discrimination. The relation between them is continuously changing in accordance with the action of karma.

Skilful means Buddhist practice of compassion in sharing the dhamma with the unenlightened. Tradition describes the Buddha explaining the Dhamma at different levels to different people. In the Lotus Sutra tricks and deceptions are among the skilful means employed to lead the lost to salvation.

Socrates (469–399 BCE) Greek philosopher and teacher and mentor of Plato. He taught by a method of question and answer which sought to elicit a consistent and rational response and hence to arrive at a universally agreed truth. He was executed in Athens for corrupting the youth and introducing strange gods.

Soka Gakkai 'Value-creating society' of lay members of the Japanese Buddhist sect Nichiren. It was founded in 1930 in a wave of new cults. It is evangelistic, exclusive, and highly organized. It runs its own political party and has schools and a university.

Sorcerer A practitioner of harmful magic. In indigenous religions sorcerers are sometimes believed to be able to kill others through magic.

Soteriology Teaching about salvation.

Soto Zen School of Zen Buddhism which teaches a gradual and gentle way to Satori.

Soul (1) The immortal element of an individual man or woman which survives the death of the body in most religious teachings. (2) A human being when regarded as a spiritual being.

Spiritualism Any religious system or practice which has the object of establishing communication with the dead.

Stupa Tibetan Buddhist shrine, found by roadsides, in fields, and at gateways. It is shaped as a pointed dome, often with a spire crescent and disc at the top, and built on a square base. The construction represents the five elements and may contain relics or images or texts of sacred scripture. Many stupas in India date from the reign of king Asoka.

Sutta Pitaka An important collection of Theravada Buddhist scriptures. It consists of sermons of the Buddha, including the Dhammapada.

Suzuki, Daisetz T. (1870–1966 CE) Japanese Zen scholar who played a major part in introducing Zen Buddhism to the Western world. He was a member of the Rinzai sect and was sympathetic to Christianity.

T

Taboo Polynesian word applied to an object, place, or person which is prohibited because of its holy or dangerous character. It may include the sense of being 'marked off' and therefore separate from everyday usage.

Tanha ('craving') The main cause of suffering as analyzed by the Buddha in the Four Noble Truths.

Tantrism Tibetan Buddhist practices which aim at direct experience of the enlightened self through symbols, visual images, repetition of sounds, prescribed movements, breath control, and ritualized sexual intercourse.

Temple Building designed for worship of God or gods, usually containing a sanctuary or holy place where sacrifice may be offered.

Tendai Japanese Buddhist sect based on a former Chinese sect T'ien-t'ai, and founded in the ninth century CE. Tendai was an attempt at a synthesis between Mahayana teachings which stressed meditation and those that stressed devotion.

Theism The belief in one supreme God who is both transcendent and involved in the workings of the universe.

Theology A systematic formulation of belief made by or on behalf of a particular individual or church or other body of believers.

Theophany A divine appearance, revelation, or manifestation, usually inducing awe and terror in those who witness it.

Theosophy ('divine wisdom') A term applied to various mystical movements but which refers particularly to the principles of the Theosophical Society founded by Madame Blavatsky in 1875. These comprise a blend of Hindu, Buddhist, and Christian ideas, together with particular stress on reincarnation, immortality, and the presence of God in all things.

Theravada ('the doctrine of the elders') The form of Buddhism practised in Sri Lanka, Myanmar (Burma), Thailand, Cambodia, and Laos, which sticks firmly to the teachings of the Vinaya Pitaka and rejects the doctrine of the bodhisattvas.

Three Body doctrine Mahayana Buddhist teaching that the Buddha exists in three

aspects. His human existence was his 'transformation body'. In his celestial existence he appears in his 'enjoyment body'. But the ultimate basis of his Buddhahood is his 'truth body' which unites all three bodies. This is identical with ultimate reality.

Three refuges Brief dedication used by Buddhists and traditionally given by the Buddha himself: 'I go to the Buddha for refuge; I go to the Dhamma for refuge; I go to the Sangha for refuge.'

Tibetan Book of the Dead Book of instructions and preparations for death and rites to be performed for the dying. In Tibetan Buddhism the dying must train in advance, helped by a spiritual teacher, to face the clear light of the Void, reality itself, in such a way as to avoid rebirth, or at least to ensure a human rebirth.

Tibetan Buddhism/Vajrayana A mixture of Buddhism, Tantrism, and the ancient Bön religion of Tibet. The two main groups are the Red Hats and the Yellow Hats. (*See also* chakras; chorten; Dalai Lama; lama; mandala; panchen Lama; prayer wheels; Tibetan Book of the Dead.)

Tipitaka The 'three baskets' of the Buddha's teaching, the canon of scripture for Theravada Buddhists, comprising the Vinaya Pitaka, the Sutta Pitaka, and the Abhdhamma Pitaka.

Transcendent That which is above or beyond common human experience or knowledge.

Tripitaka (1) Sanskrit spelling of the (Pali) word Tipitaka. (2) The scriptures of Theravada Buddhism, which include translations of Theravada texts, Sanskrit Mahayana texts, and some Chinese additions and commentaries. Also called the San-tsang.

Triple gem The Buddha as teacher, the dhamma as his teaching, and the sangha as the community who live by his teaching. The 'triple gem' is the core of the Buddhist faith.

V

Vairocana A title for the sun in ancient Hindu mythology. In Mahayana Buddhism it became a title for one of the great Buddhas. He is regarded as supreme Buddha in Java and in the Japanese Shingon sect. He was said to be identical with the Shinto sun deity Amaterasu.

Vajrayana ('diamond vehicle') An expression sometimes used for Tibetan Buddhism, a form of Mahayana Buddhism which has distinctive doctrines and practices.

Vinaya Pitaka One of the oldest Buddhist scriptures consisting of the rules of discipline for the Sangha, and related commentaries.

W

Wandering On In Buddhist thought the continual cycle by which the karma of past actions causes the coming-to-be of new mental and physical states which in turn produce more karma and further phases of existence.

World Fellowship of Buddhists Society founded in 1950 in Ceylon (Sri Lanka) by G. P. Malalasekera to bring together Buddhists of all traditions and nations with the common intention of spreading Buddhist teaching throughout the world.

Worship Reverence or homage to God or a god which may involve prayer, sacrifice, rituals, singing, dancing, or chanting.

Y

Yellow Hats Reformed branch of Tibetan Buddhism whose leader is the Dalai Lama. (*See* Buddhism.)

Z

Zen Japanese Buddhist movement which developed from the Chinese Ch'an school in the twelfth century CE. It is characterized by the teaching that enlightenment is a spontaneous event, totally independent of concepts, techniques, or rituals. Zen aims at harmony in living and uses secular arts such as tea-making and calligraphy to develop effortless skills.

Index

Numbers in **bold type** indicate pages with illustrations.
The Rapid Fact-Finder is not indexed.

Picture Acknowledgments

Dreamstime pp. 16, 29, 38, 41, 44, 75,
    85, 94

Illustrated London News pp. 13, 32

Photodisc p. 25

Photolink pp. 53, 56, 57, 63, 70, 72, 83

Tim Dowley Associates p. 35